DON'T TELL ME WHAT TO DO

The Secret Guide to Unlocking Your
Power, Potential, and Purpose

JENNIFER DUNPHY DRPH, MBA

To my children, Holden and Shepley, who I hope will be the change I want to see in the world. I love you.

Author Bio

Dr. Jennifer Dunphy is a doctor of public health and currently serves as the chief population health officer at one of California's largest healthcare organizations, responsible for delivering care to over one million members. Jennifer earned her doctorate from the University of North Carolina-Chapel Hill, her Masters of Business Administration from Loyola Marymount University, her Masters of Public Health from UC Berkeley, and her undergraduate degree in neuroscience and natural sciences from the University of Southern California.

Jennifer's public health research has been published in some of the top journals in her field, including *The American Journal of Managed Care*. She has been recognized with several national awards, including *Becker's Hospital Review's* "Top Chief Population Health Officers to Know," and *Modern Healthcare's* "Emerging Leader in Healthcare Award." Jennifer is an active advocate for all things public health on social media and has a popular monthly health newsletter with over 1,000 subscribers and growing.

Jennifer is the author of, *The Toxin Handbook*, a book that teaches chronically ill and health-conscious individuals how to eliminate dangerous toxins in the home. Jennifer regularly lectures at major conferences across the country and is the CEO and founder of a new SaaS healthcare start-up aimed at changing the way healthcare providers meet the needs of vulnerable populations.

Most importantly, Jennifer is the mom of two rambunctious boys. She resides in Orange County, California, with her husband, Taylor. Jennifer loves to ski, cook, read, and spend time with family. You can follow Jennifer @drjendunphy on Instagram, Twitter, and Facebook, and visit her on her website www.drjendunphy.com

Don't Tell Me What To Do

The Secret Guide to Unlocking Your Power, Potential, and Purpose

If you are craving more for yourself—more happiness, success, productivity, and the need to set yourself up for the best future possible—this book is for you. If you have failed before, it is now your turn to succeed. If you are someone who feels like you have more to give back to the world, the secret strategies in this book will help you quickly hone and activate your visions—turning what you thought were impossible dreams into your everyday reality.

CONTENTS

INTRODUCTION

This book is meant for those with FIRE inside of them—a burning, passionate fire for what they want to accomplish with their one life. This book is for people who have an overwhelming desire to change the world. It is for the ambitious, type A go-getters who will not settle for anything less than what they deserve. For this kind of person, their worst fear is to die without fully expressing their potential and introducing their gifts to the world. These individuals will resonate with the quote attributed to Wayne Dyer: "Don't die with your music still in you."

This person is usually described as a leader, eccentric, and wise. If this is you, you will likely have already found success in many aspects of your life but find that it isn't enough. You want more—you want to do more, help more, be more. If you are one of these people, you already know it, and this book was made for you. You are not only a part of the fire tribe, you were born a member. You can think of this book and the pages that follow as a road map to help you fan the flames and further ignite the fire already inside of you, spread it into the world, and fully become who you know you are meant to be.

If this person who I am describing is someone that you used to be, that is okay too. You still have the fire, trust me. In some of us, for various reasons, this fire burns out after childhood. But if you had it, even for a little bit, it IS still in you and has the potential to be lit again. And that is what I am here for.

There was a point in my life where I would have done anything for a book like this to help instruct me on how to reach my highest potential, and guide me through hardships, challenges, highs, and lows. I wrote this book after asking myself, if I died and I wanted to teach my children ONE thing so that they could find happiness and success in their adult lives, what would it be? This book is the answer to that question.

Before we begin, I want to make one thing clear—I genuinely believe in you, who you are and what you can do. I know you wouldn't have gotten this far and to this book if you weren't someone who has a whole lot to give back to the world.

I cannot even count the number of people throughout my life who have told me I can't do what I want to do. You can't have young kids and be a C-suite executive. You can't have a salary in the top one percent and work from home. You aren't ready to be a CEO in your thirties, no one will offer you that job. You can't have a job that is both successful and flexible. You can't be a truly present mom and a corporate fireball. You can't start your own company and have a full-time job. You can't write a book…No, nope, nah, you can't, you shouldn't, you won't.

I am here to tell you, as living proof, that you absolutely can. If you dream it, it's possible. Half the battle is convincing yourself you are worth it; the other half is going for it and not stopping until you get it. The triple threat is Confidence, Ambition, and Perseverance (CAP). I have learned that if you can cultivate those three skills (and they *are* skills)—it doesn't really matter what you do or how you do it—you will probably, eventually, succeed. Hence, billionaires being made out of people who, for example, invented the frozen burrito (not a small feat). Of course, there are technical skills, experience, timing, and good ol' luck, but I've found that those are always inferior to the triple threat of CAP.

I don't profess to know everything and I have A LOT left that I want to achieve in my life, but I wouldn't have gotten to where I am today without using the methods outlined in this book. I know what has worked for me and what has helped me attain and sustain my level of productivity and create a life I am proud of. Through experiences, trial and error, and blood, sweat and tears, I have honed these methods to work consistently and effectively. They have been my hidden secrets...until now.

I want to share what has worked for me and provided me with extraordinary results because I am confident these methods will work for you too. If you take even one small part of this book and apply it to your life, those actions will create changes, which will beget larger changes, which will have a positive ripple effect in your life and in the world.

By applying these methods, I earned a senior executive (C-suite) level promotion while pregnant (and sick), purchased my first home with money I had saved up from working, started working from home, passed my final exams for my doctoral program, wrote my dissertation (the first in my class to finish), published a research paper in a top journal, earned several awards in my industry, completed my doctorate, and more than doubled my salary—within six months. I also proved to myself what I had always known and what you now know as well: this works. At that point in my life, and because of the methods in this book, I was making actionable moves that were getting me closer to my ideal life vision. And you will too. Now, I rely on the secrets in this book daily to push me further than I ever thought was possible. Since then, I have accomplished bucket list dreams of mine within MONTHS that I originally thought would take me DECADES. I founded businesses, wrote and published multiple books, built a health brand, became a public health advisor and more...It's your turn now–this book is your step-by-step guide toward finally achieving the life YOU envision.

Designing your life starts with drawing up a blank slate and then repainting only the things you want in it. Of course, there are certain parts of your life that are unchangeable, like the fact you are based in a certain city (for now), or perhaps the fact that you had a difficult or traumatic childhood. So, when I say draw a blank slate, what I mean is this: allow for the opportunities in front of you to take any shape you want. Don't let past hardships and current limitations create unnecessary future obstacles.

The most important phase of this process is the design phase, so only design what you want to safeguard and attain. Allow all desired options to be possible, because there is a way to make them a reality.

Your ideal life vision design is the focus of the first part of this book and will be the foundation for everything that comes next. Many of the things I dreamt about weren't easy for me to achieve. If I had listened to those who told me to stay in my lane, ignore my vision, and continue to play, not small, but *appropriately*, I would have never reached where I am today. In fact, I wouldn't even be close. I don't want to be on my death bed someday saying, "wow I had a really *appropriate* life."

"Dream big" is not just a cliché phrase, it is a call-to-action that will shape your future. It is the first step in allowing yourself to transform into the best version of you.

After setting the foundation by defining your ideal life, I will walk you through the practical methods and exercises which will guide you in achieving the visions you designed.

Be aware, this book isn't about sitting on your bed "manifesting" piles of money. This book is about REAL practical tools and strategies that work. These methods were discovered through decades of exploration, practice, and diligence. These strategies have been honed and perfected, and now just by picking up this book—they are all yours.

How to read this book

Of course, you can read this book and engage in these exercises in any way that works for you, but I wanted to provide you with several recommendations that work best when diving into the material.

This book is not meant to be skipped around or skimmed through. To get the most out of this program, I recommend you read each chapter in numerical order. The chapters are arranged in a specific order, designed to guide you through a transformative process that allows you to build up a vision, then take action through practical exercises.

I have attempted to make this book as concise as possible by giving you the essential information only (I know how busy you are) without any filler. Each chapter is dense, so it may take you more time than you expected to fully process each section. As you journey through the book, read it slowly to let the information sink in and to give yourself some time to reflect on how each chapter applies to your life.

As you start to engage in the exercises, it is beneficial to give yourself at least one full day between completing each exercise before continuing with the material. This pace gives you enough time to go back and add additional information, thoughts, and insights before moving on.

It will be tempting to plow through the material, especially when you get excited (my fire people will know this feeling). I always try to complete things expeditiously, but speed isn't the goal with this book. The goal is to get through this process in an honest and comprehensive way so that the changes you enact will make a lasting and profound impact on you. To ensure that this happens, I encourage you to go back and reflect on how the work you have completed in each chapter is resonating with you—there is no way around this—this process takes time and cannot be rushed.

When it's time to move on to the next chapter and the subsequent exercises, you should feel genuinely ready to move on and learn more. If you are still caught up in an idea or a thought that you had when reading a certain chapter, or if you're still wrapped up in one of the exercises, instead of just moving on through the rest of the book, take a pause, let it sit, and then come back to it. Often, I find this iterative process brings fresh insight to a part of your vision that you weren't immediately clear on. Clarity is the goal—take as long as you need until you FEEL the clarity in your answers.

The exercises in this book and the type of thinking you are about to engage in isn't always easy. As you progress through the book, you want to feel at peace with the work you've done so far and excited about continuing the process. If you feel stressed or uneasy, that simply means you need more time to process and reflect on the current exercise or chapter. Be aware that some chapters are emotionally draining. Those portions of the book require the most from you and therefore may also require more time to mentally process and to work though. Not only is this feeling completely normal, it is expected. It means the process is working for you. You will be so glad you stuck with it. The outcome, I promise, will be worth it all.

I often find myself wanting to go back and add more after I finish an exercise because I thought of something new in the shower or in bed when my mind had a moment to quiet down and relax. This is exactly what the process is intended to look like. If that's happening to you as you work through this book, then you are on the right track.

To summarize, give yourself adequate time to complete each exercise, and then at least one additional day to think about the exercise and your answers before you move on to the next one. Your process may take longer than a day—the timeline differs for everyone.

Now with that in mind, let's get going!

If you would like to download the workbook meant to help you work through the exercises in this book you can access it for free at the following website www.drjendunphy.com/books.

PART I
THE DREAM

CHAPTER 1

THE BEGINNING

I was bossy right out of the womb. My mom loves telling the story about the time I was absolutely sure I had a headache in my back. When she tried to explain that you can't have a headache in your back, I told her she didn't know what she was talking about.

I was three.

I don't know if I was influenced more by nature or nurture, but I am your classic type A personality. This is both a blessing and a curse. This type of personality never really gets to chill out—even on vacation, and this often breeds extra stress and even anxiety. We are high-achievers, hard on ourselves, disciplined, and often, yep, a little bossy. The bossiness is usually an attempt to control ourselves and our environment. We don't like chaos, surprises, or messy environments, and we pride ourselves on being the ones who can pull the strings to effect the changes we want to make in our daily lives.

While I grew to learn that, indeed, you cannot have a headache in your back, and that other people are certainly right sometimes (especially my mother), I still have not lost that three-year-old type A spunk that drives me every day.

As I grew up and matured, I encountered more and more resistance to my ideas, ambition, and drive. As real life seeped into my fantastic dreams and tried to derail them, I became a bit disillusioned with the goals that started to sail by me as life droned on. I said to myself, "Okay, I guess I am not going to be a millionaire by twenty-five," "Alright, there goes my chance to be a neurosurgeon," "See you later, feature in Forbes 30 under 30," etc. etc. etc. Why did it all seem possible at one point, if not likely, and then slowly less possible, and then, suddenly, impossible?

We all have our own version of this. Perhaps being married with kids by thirty, or achieving certain goalposts in our career, or even becoming a movie star/famous singer/major league athlete. There is a personal flavor to this disappointment as you see your dreams narrow and hollow out, and your goals shrink like a friend waving goodbye to you in your rearview mirror.

I felt the influence of others trying to restrict my opportunities and tamper with my visions—anyone from school professors, to family and friends, to guidance counselors. Of course, there were also supporters (and I thank them for cheering me on), but the more grandiose my ideas and dreams were, the fewer supporters I found. The most ardent supporter I had, in truth, was myself. It felt lonely trying to achieve my dreams, and sometimes it still does. I often got the feeling that people wanted me to achieve "just enough" but certainly no more.

You can get stuck there, sometimes for quite a while, in that space of "just enough." Just enough starts to become a habit instead of a resting place, but for those of us with the fire inside, this space will never feel like home. It will never feel right. We know we aren't done.

Once your achievements start to break through the barriers of normalcy (which if you are reading this book, they will) there can be even more pushback in the form of, "you are taking on too much!" and, "what are you thinking?" and my personal favorite, "you can't do it all." But what people trying to achieve big dreams often don't realize is how incredibly common these types of responses are and how there's a way to fight back, shore up our remaining hope and drive, and forge a new, great path . . . a movement.

A lot of the work we are going to do will feel lonely because (at least in the beginning) it is meant to be. This process is meant to build up your inner confidence so that when you fail, when you inevitably come up against obstacles and challenges and pushback from yourself or others, when no one believes in you (because, trust me, there will be times you feel this way), you will still have a way to stoke that fire burning inside of you and persevere.

Nobody achieves lasting success alone, but we must first create an unbreakable inner foundation that allows us to be our own greatest guide. In the following chapters, we will discuss how to leap off that inner trampoline and bounce up again when you fall, how to cultivate the confidence you need to take that next step, and most importantly how to become the best version of yourself.

When I first considered becoming a doctor of public health, I had to speak with an admission counselor so that they could assess whether or not I was qualified to apply to the doctoral program. I was sitting in my car in the parking lot of a Thai food restaurant. I remember the jeans and white sweater I was wearing, the scent of yellow curry, and the pit of utter rejection I felt in my stomach when I heard those disappointing words from the admissions counselor on the other end of the phone—"If I were you, I wouldn't bother to apply to the program."

The admissions counselor went on to tell me that not only did she think I shouldn't even apply, but that if I was accepted for some reason, she didn't think I would be academically successful. Double whammy. This was her *job*, to tell people if they should apply for doctoral candidacy, and, in her expert opinion, I didn't cut it. I asked her if any elements of my history or application would preclude me from applying and she said "no," but that if she were me, she really wouldn't waste her time with the effort. She asserted that the program was simply too competitive.

This was a pivotal experience because what I had to do in that moment was to truly own my power. Only I knew what I was capable of. No one else. No matter who they were. Again, I felt like I was on an island, deserted and alone. But because I had created a pretty habitable island, I was okay with that. I had developed enough confidence within myself to break the criticism down, discard what I didn't want, take what I wanted, and push forward.

Of course, this exchange was disheartening, but I applied to the doctoral program anyway. I made sure that my application represented my potential contributions as a student and a future doctor in my field. My interviews ended up going well, and shortly after I received a letter officially stating my acceptance into the program. I was going to be a doctor.

I couldn't have been more excited, but upon meeting my fellow students, the words of the admission counselor instantly came rushing back into my mind full-speed like a freight train without breaks. I did actually feel out of my league. My colleagues were the real deal, impressive beyond measure, and this program brought out self-doubt. I was sitting next to successful medical doctors, best-selling authors, global executives, world-class researchers, public health celebrities, a leader of one of the largest non-profits in the world, and philanthropic powerhouses. These people were actually changing the world, while I was just thinking about it. Out of my league was an understatement. We had the guy to my left who managed distribution of critical medical supplies throughout Africa, and the woman to my right who spent her life researching how to save the lives of sick babies born into poverty. The woman across from me was the head of a cancer research collaborative, and the guy sitting next to her held one of the top positions at the CDC. You get the idea. Maybe the guidance counselor was right all along. Maybe my admission decision was some sort of mistake? Was I even supposed to be here?

I was. It wasn't an easy journey by any means, but I ended up finishing first in my class. I was the second-youngest person in my cohort (shout-out to my colleague Sara) and, incidentally, the only student in my class who had a baby during the course of the program (bonus points since technically we both went through the program).

I tell you this story to let you know that other people's opinions of you should never influence your own opinion of what you know to be true about yourself. This might seem simple, but it's not. My whole life was full of people telling me I couldn't do things. Unfortunately, when you dream big, very few people tell you that you can. If I had let someone else's perception of me impact what I knew I was capable of, I would have never persevered. But, because my inner-knowing was strong enough, I was able to discard the negativity and embrace my potential. It's your turn.

It is easy for people to say they are impressed and proud of you after the fact, but rare for people to believe you can achieve big outcomes before they are achieved. Find these people if you can, the ones who believe in you as much or more than you believe in yourself—they are hidden gems in your quest for greatness. If you don't have that type of person in your life yet—I am here to be your cheerleader. The cheerleader for those with BIG dreams, the ones who want to change the world, for real. I am here for those of you who want to do it all.

This book is for those of you who want to live life as fully as possible on your terms. I am also here to advocate for those of you who don't know what you want to do yet, and to tell you this: anything is possible. I am here to say, **YES, YOU CAN**.

The power you have is unimaginable, and in the following pages, I will give you the tools and strategies for claiming that power, step-by-step.

I have been constantly underestimated. I have been underestimated because I am a female, I am small, I don't have a booming voice, and I am not six foot tall with broad shoulders. I also don't "make sense" to a lot of people. I love fashion and academics, *The Real Housewives* and classic literature, parties and computer programming. I have a serious job, but my favorite activity is laughing. My genuine self is silly—really silly. Dancing around with my kids, making up songs, and practical jokes are the norm in my house. However, I spend my days helping very sick people get the healthcare they need—which is no laughing matter. I was also on a hit reality TV show for six years throughout high school and college, which made it even more common for people to underestimate me. I've spent my whole life hearing comments like "I didn't know you were smart," and "oh, look at Jen Bunney (my maiden name)—she's a DOCTOR?"

Why am I telling you this and why does it matter? I finally realized it isn't MY job to make sense to anyone, and to achieve success I've had to be careful about whose voices I listen to and which voices I choose to believe and internalize. I don't fit a common mold, and I would bet, since you're reading this book, that you might feel the same way. Not fitting a common mold can make people feel uncomfortable because people tend to love predictability and labels. They want to define you as an academic, or as lazy, or as introverted or hedonistic—you name it. Once they label you, you only get advice relevant to that label. And that's the dangerous part.

I've had to learn to trust my own voice, always. Whenever I don't trust my own voice, I inevitably get into trouble. As I have gained a diversity of experience, I have learned to hone and refine that voice. Now when I hear advice, even from an expert or professed guru, I stop and ask myself, "Does this resonate with me, with my experiences, with my goals?" If the answer is no, I say, "Thank you for your thoughts," and I go on my way. I am also very careful with who I ask for advice from because at the end of the day, if you rely on any advice too heavily, it can drown out your own instincts and become a breeding ground for doubt and uncertainty.

Our instincts, together with the "knowing" of our ultimate inner potential, is one of the most powerful tools we have.

How you take advice from others is a critical part of being successful. Every piece of advice comes from someone else's lived experiences, through their eyes, not yours. And even the best intended advice givers may not have your lofty goals and visions in mind. I often find, on average, that external advice trends towards pushing me to play small, while my internal voice says bigger, more, you got this.

Once I asked a close friend how much money I should ask for during an upcoming promotion at one of my former jobs. This person could not possibly have known my potential and the value I had to offer, but at that point, my tenuous self-confidence still pushed me to seek outside advice. The individual gave me a number they thought I should aim for. The number was reasonable and made sense according to their experience. However, I knew that even a good market reference value could be misleading because then you end up comparing your value to others perceived value instead of valuing yourself based on your unique contributions. My worth likely equated to double the proposed salary, if not triple, and I had a value proposition to back up why. I lovingly ignored my friend who gave me the advice, and instead went with my gut—asking for a number triple what my friend thought I was worth. It worked.

Had I listened to the advice that afternoon, I would be making a lot less money and probably be several pegs down in my career. This was a person I trusted with my life and had every reason to trust them in this scenario, but, sometimes, you have to listen only to your voice. Here's my point: you are the only one that can define your value. You and only you know your true worth.

CHAPTER 2

AWARENESS

The first step in building the life of your dreams is awareness. You need to be aware of what you currently believe about yourself and start critically questioning your negative assumptions (everyone has at least a few), even the ones you think are both true and realistic. The kind of assumptions I am talking about are the ones that start with, "I am not the kind of person that . . ." You can fill in the blanks with unlimited examples.

Here are a few of the common negative assumptions that people believe about themselves: I am not the kind of person that gets high-paying jobs, interviews well, speaks in public, wakes up early, is positive, gets into good schools, likes to work out, can make money, eats healthy, sleeps at night, engages in small talk, keeps a partner interested, can focus, can write, is attractive, is good at math, is lucky, is smart. Usually, these beliefs tend to aggregate around one category, such as body image/physical attributes, social confidence, career, intelligence, physical skills (athleticism), health/ mental health, or money.

The truth is, you can become ANY type of person you want to be; however, those negative assumptions and beliefs limit your ability to do so.

How do negative beliefs get started, and then reinforced? Many people do not realize that a good portion of our self-limiting beliefs actually originate from lack of exposure. If you have never skied, for example, you might say, "I am not a mountain person." If you have never taken calculus with a teacher that matches your learning style, you might think that the subject is too complicated for you and therefore you are "not a math person." These generalizations we so easily make can be harmful because they may or may not be accurate, yet we are often quick to make them, stick to them, and continually reinforce them.

Lack of exposure is a common root cause for some of the negative assumptions we have about ourselves. The people who hate to fly are also usually the people who don't fly very much, and so it becomes a self-perpetuating cycle. People who aren't active usually don't like to exercise, but exercising (and getting fit and good at it) makes you want to exercise more.

We often imagine we dislike something or aren't good at it as a way to re-enforce our negative beliefs without having any real evidence to back them up. Sometimes the more we do something, the better we get at it and the more we find ways to enjoy it. Consequently, that skill ends up becoming a *positive* belief about ourself instead of a negative one.

It is easy for us to say we can't do something, aren't good at it, or don't like something when we aren't exposed to it enough. Simply knowing that this phenomenon occurs will be important in helping you discover your negative assumptions. We want to constantly question whether or not a negative assumption may just be an exposure issue, and to think carefully about which negative assumptions you might be able to convert to positive ones with additional exposure and practice.

In order to challenge our assumptions, we need to understand how and where they hide. Personally, I have always thought of myself as the type of person who breaks down under pressure and who cannot handle certain high-stake situations. I have a long list of examples that seemed to confirmed my inherent weakness:

During my first public speaking engagement in front of one hundred fifty people, my hands shook so tumultuously that even the podium seemed nervous. I could hardly talk because my voice was shaking as well. I could tell everyone in the audience felt sorry for me, as if they wanted to say "it's okay", but there was nothing I could do in the moment to calm myself down. I avoided public speaking for a long time after that incident—deciding it just "wasn't my thing."

I used to suddenly begin losing at any high-pressure sports game I was initially winning at. I remember I was winning all of the matches for my high school varsity tennis tryouts, and then I started…losing. I ended up getting so nervous about my wins that I started losing all subsequent games. I ended up not even making it onto the JV team even though I'd practiced for months and had the skills to excel. I knew I could have won those games, but seeing the reaction on the other players face of "Wow, I didn't know she was any good", made me feel like I shouldn't be good and so I played to the expectations of other people instead of playing to my capabilities.

I had to void the medical school entrance exam (MCAT), which I'd spent months studying for, twice in a row, because of panic attacks. The panic would start when I came to a question I didn't know the answer to. I would be flooded with self-doubt so intense that I froze. I would physically freeze (couldn't speak or move) for so long that the time to complete the test section would be over and with only a portion of questions answered. Knowing my score would be too low, my only option was to void the test. This happened several times, reinforcing my inability to perform under pressure once again.

I quit sailing (even though I was very good at it) because the pressure at the beginning of the race was too stressful for me to handle. I remember the race committee used to honk a big horn if your boat went over the starting line too early, which would result in a penalty. The problem was that were so many boats in a small area that it was almost impossible to control my boat when the wind was strong. If my sail picked up a gust of a wind, my boat would fly in one direction with little warning. To avoid slamming into another boat and making someone *very* angry, I occasionally had to go over the starting line... "BEEEEEEEEP", "PENALTY." Sailing ended abruptly for me.

I wanted to be a medical doctor, but I wasn't able to cope with medical emergencies (needing to leave the room, feeling faint) death, or gore. One day at Tufts University in Boston they took the pre-med class to tour the medical school, at the end of tour they took us to a "special room" without telling us what was in the room or what we were doing. I quickly figured out by the smell alone that we had been ushered into a room of dead corpses. Half-dissected dead corpses. The rest of the pre-med class was so excited you would think it was Christmas morning. One kid even asked if he could "touch it." I literally ran out of the room, and sat in the hall fighting a panic attack for the next 30 minutes. I felt like I was different. I thought that this must mean the other kids were meant to be doctors and I wasn't. Knowing I would have to dissect dead bodies in medical school and deal with death daily became my biggest obstacle in deciding if I wanted to become a medical doctor. I wish I knew then, what I know—I am not a person that was "not made to be a doctor"—I just hadn't yet learned the secret of exposure.

The list goes on, and as my list lengthened, my opportunities narrowed. Whenever something like the above examples occurred, I would use it as confirmation that I "just wasn't that type of person." I lost confidence to cope with even small pressures. Not only did those experiences brand me as that type of person in my own powerful mind—nervous, weak, different, defunct, unable to succeed under pressure—they also served as reminders every time I would try to break out of the mold. They kept me down. They kept me playing small.

Finally, I learned the secrets I am going to teach to you now, and everything in my life changed.

I started questioning my assumptions, just like I am challenging you to do. I realized the problem, and it wasn't me, it was my exposures. In my life at the time, I didn't have the opportunity to deal with pressure every day. I simply did not have enough practice dealing with high intensity situations (or dead bodies) in real life. So, how did I really know I wasn't good at the things I was failing at? I didn't. In fact, I had evidence in the OPPOSITE direction.

Perhaps I would be a great ER physician, a pro-tennis player, a sailboat racer, a pilot or even an astronaut with a couple years of practice—I certainly didn't have much evidence to prove that I wouldn't be. But my negative assumptions became firm, unassailable truths I was believing about my core capabilities, and these assumptions drove some major life decisions. And it wasn't someone else making these determinations, it was me. How unfair.

It took me many years and a lot of self-reflection to recognize I was actually scared of my own success and strength. I always thought that my inability to deal with stressful situations was because I wanted success so badly that the pressure led to a breakdown. While that may be partially true, the real reason was that I had been viewing those achievements as beyond who I was at the moment. I had trouble imagining myself as the person on a competitive, award-winning varsity team, or the person who scored perfectly on the MCAT and got into my first-choice medical school, or the person who got a standing ovation from a public speaking engagement, or the person who could calmly act in an emergency.

I viewed those experiences as outside of myself instead of as a part of who I already was. If I had gone into each of those scenarios with the belief that these weren't only goals I could achieve, but that I was ALREADY the type of person who would make those achievements likely, then the outcomes would have been radically different.

I exposed myself to several of those situations over the next few years again and again. While I still get a little queasy watching people get operated on (couldn't shake this one), I can deal with emergencies, take tests like a pro, and speak in front of thousands. All because I re-defined my assumptions about what type of person I was. Now, it's your turn.

There is no question that what we believe about ourselves, if negative, can limit opportunities AND limit failures. Failures, because we can't fail if we are too scared to try. Failures are equally as important in becoming successful; if we don't take risks, we won't fail, if we don't fail, we can't learn, and if we can't learn, we won't succeed.

In the next few chapters, I am going to show you exactly how I overcame my negative assumptions about myself and how you can successfully do the same.

Can you think of points in your life where you failed at something that was really important to you?

Do you remember how those failures reinforced the negative things you believed about yourself? Almost proving them to be true?

Awareness of those assumptions is the starting point because once we're aware these assumptions exist, we can question and then challenge them. I am not talking about tricking yourself into believing something new; this is about truly taking a more balanced view of your capabilities—and thus the possibilities and opportunities that may follow.

In my life, I started asking myself the below questions:

- Are there any times I did WELL under pressure?
- What did that look like?
- Are there people just like me with some of the same constraints I have (such as anxiety) who are succeeding where I am failing? Why is that?
- When did I start believing I couldn't handle high-pressure situations?
- Is it possible what I believe is not even true?

These questions opened up a whole new world for me, and I can bet they will for you too. The next exercise will help you start deeply exploring and breaking down the negative biases you have about yourself.

Exercise 1: Revealing Biases

Fill out the below questions to the best of your ability. Take your time. There is no right or wrong answer, as long as you're honest.

Quickly make a list of all of the beliefs you have about yourself that have hindered your possible successes:

Now trash this list. Yes, you read that correctly. This set of beliefs, the ones on the first list, are not the ones we want—these are usually our superficial negative assumptions. This first list includes the assumptions we aren't afraid to admit to ourselves. Even if we change these assumptions, other ones will pop up because we aren't getting to the core.

Now, here is the hard part, make a second list. This list goes a lot deeper and will take more time. It goes past what you see and allows you to recognize unconscious biases—the ones that we don't even know we have because they are hiding from us, deeply buried. These are the biases that are driving our behavior, and they are quite insidious due to their hidden nature.

If you have trouble accessing these negative assumptions, start here:

Think of one of the things you wanted most in your life and didn't get. Why didn't you get it?

Your first thought (**the excuse**) will usually be something like "it was unfair," or "they were biased," or "it was their fault." This first answer usually involves blaming of some kind (this is a completely normal defense mechanism—we just have to drive past it). Ask yourself again.

What was something you really wanted and didn't get? The second answer (**the superficial bias**) normally turns the spotlight back around on us, but still tends to cover up the deeper negative beliefs we have—it doesn't get to the truth.

We often don't want to bring the deeper assumptions into the light, so we make up something easier to digest (which may be partially true), to continue hiding the real, more painful underlying belief (the deeper bias). The **deeper bias** is beneath **the excuse** and the **superficial bias**—you know you have hit it when it hurts. This is the one you want. We can make this ugly belief beautiful by turning vulnerability into strength.

Below is an example:

The situation: My partner broke up with me.

The excuse: They don't know what they want in life, they're immature, they will never commit.

The superficial bias: I can't pick good partners.

The DEEPER bias: I am not interesting or attractive enough, and I will not be able to keep a loving partner, which means I will always be alone. I believe I am unlovable.

You can see how, in this example, the hidden negative belief doesn't necessarily come first, and it may be more difficult to unearth. But that is the belief we need to get to and uncover in order to make progress. Usually, every time something negative happens that is related to the belief (in this example, with a partner), we tend to reinforce it and let it grow stronger, using new events as "evidence" that the belief is true. We might also continue to cover up the underlying belief with the same superficial excuses.

By the way, in this example the "real" reason your partner broke up with you is completely irrelevant to your work and progress, we are just using emotional events in life to get to the core of what you believe about yourself. Remember, in order to combat these beliefs, we have to recognize them. It might be painful to do so, but once you do you will feel relief as well, because now we can work on exploring them.

Since I am asking you to do this hard work, I will share a personal example of working through this exercise myself.

The situation: I didn't get into medical school my first time applying, even though I applied to forty-five schools and studied for this my whole life. (The acceptance into medical school had been a dream of mine since I was a child.)

The excuse: The medical school entrance exam was unfair. The testing environment was distracting. It was too hard in areas that I am not as strong in.

The superficial bias: I am not a good test taker because of my anxiety.

The DEEPER bias: I am not as smart as the rest of my family, who are all physicians. I will not fit in with my family. I am not like everyone else in my family. I am not good enough.

Thankfully, I now know that none of that is true, but I spent a long time believing it, and I had to uncover my hidden biases in order to confront these negative assumptions.

Be aware that not all negative assumptions are necessarily hidden. Some are out in the open. If they are out in the open, we tend to talk about them regularly, and often with self-deprecation. However, the beliefs which we do not talk about are the ones that are most toxic to our well-being and most harmful to our future success. This is why it is so important to attempt this exercise in order to discover yours.

Go through this exercise (situation, excuse, superficial bias, deeper bias) as many times as you are willing with different situations to generate your **DEEPER BIAS** list. This is the second list and the one we will work with in the next exercise. This **DEEPER BIAS** list will likely touch difficult emotions such as loss/grief, shame/regret/guilt, disappointment/frustration, sorrow/sadness, pain/hurt/frustration. That is okay. It means you are doing this exercise correctly, because the most challenging times in our life are also the ones where our negative beliefs tend to surface the most.

Once we establish awareness of these beliefs, we can start to explore the innermost depth of the person we have painted ourselves to be. In the next exercise, we begin to start loosening the grip these assumptions have on our life.

Exercise 2: Exploring Assumptions

Fill out these questions for each negative belief you uncover. Do not rush this exercise, it is pivotal to where we are going next.

- Assume for a second your negative belief is true, what exactly makes it true? Provide facts and data only—no opinions, guesses or assumptions.

- Was this negative belief always true?

- If not, when did it become true? (Be specific—name an event, an age, or a day/year.)

- Were there any times that your beliefs proved not to be true?

- If so, describe those instances.

- Is there a possibility for the opposite of your negative assumption to be true some of the time? Imagine what this looks like in detail. Write it down.

- What might it look like if the opposite of your negative assumption were true MOST of the time? What would change?

Check each deeper bias one at a time, asking yourself these questions, and see if you feel some of your negative beliefs start to lose their grip on you. Once you can prove to yourself there might possibly be some holes in your logic, you will see holes everywhere. Even if you break just one of them down a little bit—perhaps by admitting, "Okay, this belief is not ALWAYS true"—you will start to loosen them all up. This process is kind of like loosening a tight knot in a necklace; at first the knot looks so tight you think there's no way you could break it up, but once you start poking at it, it inevitably becomes easier and easier to untangle—and suddenly all the knots fall away.

This process may go slowly, it might take some time to start untangling the complex webs of assumptions we have spent years training ourselves to believe. But, if you continue this exercise regularly and apply it to every situation in which your unconscious (now turned conscious) belief emerges, you will start seeing yourself in a whole new light.

CHAPTER 3

CONFIDENCE AND
TRIGGERS

We all have areas of life where we lack a sense of internal value. In these areas, we tend to be a bit more sensitive to criticism, failure, and judgment. Some lack confidence in social situations. For others, their lack of confidence comes out in relationships or intimacy. For others still, it might involve issues regarding performance at work.

Awareness of these areas is key, because where we have low confidence, we usually have triggers. To be productive, healthy, and happy, we have to learn how to cope with these triggers. Failing to cope with triggers can lead to volatile relationships, internal strife, and an overall more stressful existence. Because we all have triggers, learning to cope with them is one of the first steps I recommend when starting to actively build your version of the life you want.

Triggers typically stem from the wounds of past trauma, which left untreated, can invade both the present and future. The importance of this cannot be overstated and that is why I have devoted an entire chapter to addressing them.

Triggers can be anything from certain topics to specific people or situations which cause us considerable distress and even anger because they tend to unearth our insecurities and disappointments. Usually, we don't understand what touches a nerve or why, and our first reaction is to immediately blame the other person or situation (whether or not blame is deserved is beside the point). We can only control ourselves and our reactions, so, reacting to the people who set off our triggers does little to help us move forward. Therapy, journaling, and talking it out with a close friend can help uncover the reasons why we are emotionally provoked by certain situations, people, words, or specific comments.

On the surface, triggers can seem so inexplicable that even the person experiencing one may feel it is nonsensical. There are contradictions everywhere, but I am confident that examining your most deep-seated wounds will lead to self-mastery, with or without someone else's understanding of them. The important discovery is developing awareness of your triggers and figuring out why they occur so you can learn how best to cope with them.

My Triggers

Personally, I tend to be sensitive regarding comments about my parenting style—particularly if they revolve around me not doing something in particular, or not doing enough in general. This is probably a bad topic to be triggered by, because if you are a parent yourself, or if you're friends with someone who is a parent, you know that everyone has an opinion on this topic, from close family members to complete strangers. For me, it took a lot of work using the techniques in this chapter to uncover the underlying reasons why that topic in particular bothered me so much, and then all the pieces came together and it finally made sense.

Because of my challenging entry into motherhood due to health complications and a difficult labor, I was unable to do the simple things I wanted to do with my baby. I became very insecure regarding my role as a first-time mother. So, when others made negative or suggestive comments on the topic of motherhood, the pain was so specific, it felt pointed directly at my psyche.

For example, people close to me were saying things like, "you don't spend enough time with your son," and, "if you want to work and have kids, you need to get up early and do more." A lot of "you don't…" and "you need to…" comments concerning how I raise my children. I feel a lot of judgment in this area. But truth be told, there is probably equal judgment happening in other areas of my life, and the reason I don't notice it is because it doesn't get my attention and trigger my emotions like comments about my children do. Capturing your attention and emotions is what defines a trigger.

Another trigger for me is when a doctor says, "Well this might be more serious and I want to rule out X (enter in any disease), so let's just check it out with these tests." It isn't the doctor's fault—it's mine. Naming any particular disease puts me into a panicked tailspin. I am triggered by health issues because I view them as huge threats to my family's well-being, and I blame myself for not being able to prevent illness (over-responsibility). I used to think I would feel terribly guilty if I ever got seriously ill, thus any health-related, potentially negative news was a huge trigger for me.

I share these personal triggers with you to let you know we all have them, and that you don't have to apologize for the things that trigger you—it is just the way you are. And the whole you (including your triggers) is valuable and worthwhile. Some of us only have a handful of triggers, while some of us may have more. But I often notice that many triggers overlap. We usually have a set of a few primary triggers that just repeat themselves and show up in different forms. Mine, for example, are mostly around being a good and responsible person.

Because we all have triggers, we need to learn to work with them so that we can cope more effectively and keep them from getting in the way of our happiness, health, productivity, and relationships.

The first step toward this goal is awareness, and the second step is recognizing the moment when you are elevated to a space driven by fear.

When you feel that trigger emotion coming out to play, STOP whatever you are doing. It doesn't matter if the trigger is someone's fault or if you are overreacting (which can be common with triggers). Overreacting does not have to mean overreacting outwardly. Overreacting can be an internal emotional response that's bigger than you might have in a similar situation but with a non-triggering topic/person. Overreacting also doesn't mean that your response (internal or external) is inappropriate or unwarranted in any way—it just means that if the topic were not your emotional bullseye, your response would be, on average, less intense.

It is also very natural to want to blame someone immediately. That's a completely normal response. But assigning fault is completely irrelevant for this step; we aren't adjudicating, we're just becoming aware. The only goal is to recognize that you are being triggered.

Once you realize you're being triggered, do something to mark your awareness. Say to yourself, "This is it. I am in the middle of being triggered right at this very moment." You can even have a designated trigger paper, where you draw a red X every time you are triggered to physically mark the event.

After you become aware, the goal is to not emotionally dive into the situation—like into a soft bed at the end of a long day—it will be very tempting to do so. Instead, you want to try to immediately (or as soon as you possibly can) change your environment and the scene in your mind so that you aren't grabbed (emotionally) by whatever is going on. Some examples of activities that you can do to create space between you and your trigger are to leave the room, exercise, watch a favorite show, or read—anything that works for you to get your brain's attention to fully switch to a different channel. If you only commit to a change in activity but do not commit to refreshing your mindset, it will not have the intended effect. You need to select an activity that completely transitions your attention to another object.

If you need more space than the few hours a new activity can provide, I recommend travel. Travel gets you out of your environment and changes it completely. Of course, it is completely unrealistic to travel with every trigger (especially with expenses, and for some, family and work), but if you have just gone through a particularly intense event, or if you've been triggered for a long period of time, it is definitely a strategy I recommend. Once you experience new places and see how other people live (even for a day), you are likely to gain a new perspective on your issues, almost like looking at planet Earth from space. Distance helps you realize how infinitesimally small we are and creates a lot of room between you and your immediate issues.

Any space you can create (the more the better) between you and your trigger will help you in coping, both short and long term. You'll be better able to process your trigger in the following step, and then you will be able to do it again next time you are triggered, which sets you up for long-term success.

Remember, when it involves a trigger, make the space bigger!

Let me explain why space is so vital. Triggers are unique. They have a special ability to continue upsetting you over the long term any time you think about them; even reflecting on past triggers can cause us to become physiologically and emotionally heightened. While disagreements and arguments on non-triggering topics normally fade in intensity over time, trigger emotions tend to stick around and can very easily re-emerge. I know people who can remember exact conversations regarding trigger situations ten years later, while the same people have a non-trigger argument with their spouse and don't even remember what they were arguing about the following week. That is the difference between a run-of-the-mill argument and a real trigger. Consequently, whenever you think about a trigger, you will tend to be, yep, triggered. Space is the antidote, and it usually is the best place to start in breaking the hold triggers have on our emotions. Triggers have the ability to get in the way of a lot of the things we are trying to achieve in this book, which is why it's important to recognize and attend to your triggers BEFORE designing your dream life.

To summarize these first steps, the goal is not to become initially baited when triggered, and we accomplish this through changing the channel in our brain by fully engaging in another activity. This strategy seems to be the only technique that works for me in the face of a genuine trigger. We want to know when we're triggered—so that we're aware it is happening—but not to get pulled into the messiness of our initial knee-jerk response. It might feel good to give in and react at first, but it is always worth it to resist.

After we give ourselves that initial space (hopefully as soon as possible after our buttons have been pushed), we are ready for the second step: a special journaling technique that I call "free pages" which allows your brain to process emotions. I recommend when journaling with this technique (described below) that you write at least a page. The reason for writing at least a page is that when we start journaling, we're usually just telling the story of what happened, but we can't access the emotional part of the *why*, or the root-cause, until we are able to process our version of what happened. I find that it takes at least a page of writing to access the point of being able to start processing emotions and dive into the *why* regarding the intensity of my feelings instead of just explaining how upset I am.

Free pages is a technique that I discovered through trial, error, and online research. It allows you to write whatever you want and truly express yourself. This very simple journaling strategy is helpful when you are feeling overwhelmed and need to make sense of an emotional trigger. I highly recommend that you only write by hand, that you write for as long as it takes for you to fill up a page (or two), and that you destroy whatever it is you have written (this is a very important step).

Journaling by hand has two purposes. The first is that writing by hand allows your brain to process emotions and thoughts more comprehensively than typing. Some theorize that because it usually takes you longer to write a word than it does to type one, you are able to more fully work through the emotion that comes along with your written words. The second reason for writing on a piece of paper with a pen is that you don't have to worry about anyone finding your writing if you physically destroy it afterwards.

Of course, on a computer or a phone there are always passwords, but passwords can easily be hacked. Furthermore, a lot of various writing programs save what you have written. For example, Microsoft Word always saves a "backup" version to recover documents in the event you accidentally delete something important and want to restore it. Google Drive has a similar feature that saves different versions of your document and stores them even if you initially delete them. The iPhone Notes app has the ability to save deleted notes and save them to your email server as well. While these features are excellent for work projects, they aren't great for disclosing your most personal and private thoughts.

For all of these reasons, typing personal thoughts and feelings on a computer makes me feel more vulnerable than when I write them down on paper knowing the document will be immediately and irrevocably destroyed. I have a small paper shredder (I highly recommend purchasing one yourself—it doesn't have to be fancy), and after I write my free pages journal entry, I shred it up into little bitty pieces. I have to admit it is quite a satisfying experience.

Often, when we think of journaling, we think of keeping what we journal about in a diary that allows us to go back and re-read it later. That is the opposite of what we are trying to achieve with this technique. The ability to re-access those words creates an instant protective filter in our minds—the exact filter we are trying to avoid. Just knowing it is possible someone else could find and read our entry or we could judge our own writing later on puts our brain out of the vulnerable space we need it to be in for this strategy to work. With free pages, it is critical that this filter is completely removed. It is liberating, even exhilarating, to be able to bare your soul and admit to things on paper that we only let ourselves think (sometimes even subconsciously)—and then destroy it.

This journaling technique is meant to help you process complex feelings. Once you are able to get your thoughts on paper, your emotions and thoughts become less alarming, scary, and intense; they might even start to make more sense to you. In using this journaling method, you have the freedom to say whatever you want about your trigger events in your free pages journal because you know it will be destroyed and no one will ever read it. This will help you process your trigger without any filter. I always feel such a sense of relief whenever I do this type of journaling and I recommend anyone working on building their ideal life engage in regular free page journaling, even when something major isn't happening in your life.

It may be the case, on occasion, that some triggers (or the cause of them) just need to be removed from your life altogether. For example, if someone is continually triggering me, I will have a serious conversation with them about my boundaries. If they continue to bring out my triggers, I will re-evaluate if that relationship is a healthy one to continue.

Since trigger emotions, new and old, have the tendency to re-emerge when you are reminded about the triggering event (even if you initially processed them through creating space and journaling), I've developed a simple technique for dealing with memories of trigger events. To do this, each primary trigger receives a symbol. So, for example, I represent the trigger of parenting criticism with a bicycle. Please note, this does not work in the moment when I am triggered, it only works when I am reminded of a past trigger event that has already occurred. Instead of engaging in those re-emerging emotions, I dive into a visualization where I imagine myself on a shore. The symbol of the trigger (in this example, the bicycle) sails by me on a boat. The bicycle on the boat continues to sail out of my view until I can no longer see it. It is very simple, but this technique allows my trigger emotions to go "out to sea" when they re-emerge after a past event.

These are the most effective techniques I have found to deal with major triggers, and I hope learning these techniques helps you more effectively (and peacefully) build the life of your dreams.

CHAPTER 4

INFLUENCES

I want you to stop and remember something: You are amazing. You have unlimited power. Your job in this world is to own your unlimited power.

We must be intentional about claiming our power and worth. As much as I would like to believe the opposite, my experiences have shown me that many people, forces, and institutions are positioned to either implicitly or explicitly take away some of our power, to get us to conform and fall in line, to remain average.

I see this insidious influence *every single day*. I see this when I observe young women apologizing when advocating for themselves in salary negotiations because it makes the other person uncomfortable. I see this when I realize that moms actually believe what their community is telling them about not being able to do it all. I see this when I notice people with SO much potential continually coloring within the lines because it's safe and familiar and they want to be perceived as "behaving well."

The influences that change our behavior can be very subtle, but subtle can be incredibly powerful. Influences may be something as simple as societal pressure which pushes us toward making a decision about how and where we should live. Sometimes the influence is simply not having enough reason to do anything different, and to just "fall into" a certain aspect of our life, such as a career or a partner. Being comfortable in and of itself can be considered an influence. Anything that creates inertia and forces back on our movement and action is an influence.

The next exercise will help you uncover how influences in your life have shaped you.

Exercise 3: Influences

As you have hopefully seen so far, one major goal of this book is to give you back the control that should be yours, so that you are living your life on your terms, without apologies.

The first step in breaking free is to become aware of the influences (both obvious and subvert) that guide your decision-making and behaviors. Once you are aware of these influences, they will exert less control over you.

Before you begin, it is important to note that when some people start answering these questions, they are taken aback by how FEW of the major decisions that have shaped their life they've actually made for themselves. If this is you, it can be startling, but don't be alarmed. This will be the beginning of taking the control back into your own hands. It is very important when answering these questions to be completely honest with yourself so that you can recognize some of the influences in your life that have shaped where you are today.

Keep in mind, not all influences are bad; some are really good. But we want to be aware of what exactly is driving our behavior either way. That's why recognizing these influences is such an important step in designing your ideal life.

To start recognizing the large and small influences in YOUR life, answer the following questions:

1. How did you decide to live where you live? (Was it because your family or a partner was living there? Did you go to school there? Relocate for a job? Did you intentionally choose your location for a clear reason?)

2. What do you spend your days doing? Did you intentionally choose that career/lifestyle or did it just happen?

3. What are some things you once hoped you would do/accomplish/experience/see but did not? What ended up getting in your way?

4. Are there any traditions/activities you participate in within your community or home that you don't believe are valuable or that you don't want to engage in but do anyway because it is easier and everyone else is doing it? (This could be anything from wearing certain clothes, spending your money in a specific way, talking about certain subjects, or anything else that allows you to conform but that doesn't resonate with you personally.)

5. How did you decide what to study in school, if you attended? (Was it what you were interested in or what someone told you to do?)

6. If you are married or in a relationship, where did you meet your partner?

7. How did you decide what political party to be affiliated with? What about your religion, if you are religious? Did you decide your political party or religion independently?

Nine times out of ten we select the person we marry based on the availability of the individuals within a five-mile radius of where we live or where we go to school/work. So, if that's true, did we really CHOOSE the person or did our location somewhat choose them for us. This may not be true for you, particularly with the advent of dating apps in the last ten years, but location has more power over us than we could ever imagine. Thus, where we live is one element we want to be very intentional about.

If you were surprised by any of your answers, you are NOT alone. For example, I am a complete product of my parents. I am not immune to these influences, but I am aware of them. My parents are X political party and Y religion, and so am I. This is not a bad thing. In fact, it's completely natural. But if you ask me if I chose those things—intentionally and independently—I would answer, "Partially, in the sense that I decided those affiliations worked for me as an adult." The honest truth is that I was completely and utterly influenced to "choose" them.

I share this to illustrate that our environment and upbringing often shape our choices dramatically, and we don't even know it. It doesn't make it right or wrong, but it does illustrate how few big decisions we really make on our own. Wouldn't you like to take that power back? I would.

Feel free to add any additional questions to this exercise regarding influences in your life that might hold relevance for you. The purpose of this exercise is not to discover every single influence you have been affected by. Instead, this exercise is meant to foster an awareness that you ARE being and have been influenced by these factors so that as you continue to move through life, you become more aware of and question these influences before they impact your major decisions.

The Antidote

If YOU aren't making a decision, then something or someone else is, *all the time*. I call that a default decision. Default decisions run lives. There are even some people who make so many default decisions that they turn into default people, where most of their life is decided by someone else. Do you know anyone like this?

The antidote to being influenced is intentionality. The more intentionality you can weave into your life, the more you will own your life, and the more your life will truly be your own. Owning your power and continually "waking up" so that you can be intentional sounds basic, but there is a genuine, and life-changing call-to-action in that message. We are all influenced by something, that's natural. But, by working on becoming aware of these influences we can begin to create a life that is extra special—a life that is uniquely ours.

I didn't really choose what I wanted to study (it was based on my desire to become a doctor, since I come from a family of physicians), where I went to college (I was a legacy at Tufts), or where I wanted to live (I decided to move home, closer to where my parents were located). Those circumstances then dictated the rest of my life—who I married, my kids, my friends, my job, etc. I estimate that I independently chose about ten percent of my life, and sadly enough this happens to most of us.

But the good news is that once you become truly aware of who and what is influencing the major decisions in your life, you can make some big changes if you want. Intentionality is like the difference between living in a model home versus a custom-built home. Of course, you cannot be intentional about absolutely everything, but the more awareness you can cultivate, the better.

Major life decisions such as where you live, work, and play, and who you associate with will ultimately shape the course of your life, so make sure you are fully present and intentional about what you want when it comes to these pivotal decisions, starting now.

CHAPTER 5

CLARITY

Now that you have established awareness of your underlying assumptions, triggers, and influences—the hardest steps—it is time to start working on clarity. Clarity means getting an idea of the direction you want your life to go in, specifically for the things that matter most to you. It means becoming clear on big picture items so that you don't let life just happen around you. It does not involve knowing all of the details.

I have developed a Clarity Guide, which I have used to obtain some amazing results and I am going to share it with you in this chapter. I used these questions to develop my own path—in part so I wouldn't be left with regrets. It helps to review your answers to these questions once every year because your values and priorities will change and shift with age and experience. This is also the part of the book where you might want to go back and share some of these answers with a current or potential life partner when you're done. Let's dive in.

Exercise 4: Clarity Guide

Think about (and write down) your answers to the below questions. These are big, important topics, so make sure you are in a calm, grounded state of mind before embarking on this exercise.

1. What is personally important for you to accomplish before you die?

These answers can encompass both big and small events. You don't have to write down items like win the Nobel Peace Prize (although, if that's your dream, go ahead), it can be as simple as wanting to spend more time with your family.

2. What type of contributions do you want to make in the world?

These answers can include anything from raising happy, healthy children, to volunteering, to making your friends laugh. Of course, your answer can also include things like inventing a new technology, advancing scientific research, or creating music and poetry! The only rule is that whatever you write down should feel like it represents you.

3. Is establishing a legacy important to you?

The overall idea of a legacy is that you are leaving something behind to help or inform future generations. Your legacy could be anything from leaving your kids an inheritance, to philanthropy, to property, to contributions to a specific field, to writing a book that future generations can read. My grandmother left behind a beautiful collection of poems and books including, *Everything by Heart* by Nora Null Bunney, for her grandchildren to read. After her memory inevitably fades, this collection of her writing will become her legacy.

Legacies are very personal. Most people think legacies have to be financial, but they can be anything that outlives you. In a way, a legacy leaves part of you in the world even though you aren't there anymore. People often tell me they think of what they want their legacy to be too late. Thinking about your legacy will help you establish clarity by eliminating the superficial and focusing on what you want people to know or remember about you in the future.

JENNIFER DUNPHY DrPH, MBA

They say we usually don't know our great grandparents' names, which means that memories of us, as humans, normally only last three to four generations. So, if you want to leave something permanent behind, it's an important thing to think about. Thinking about my legacy and how I can make a lasting positive impact is one of the questions that has helped me obtain the most clarity in my life.

4. What type of relationships do you want to have in the different stages of your life? (A partnership? Life-long friendships? Children?)

This question should not incorporate what has happened in the past, but what you want to happen in an ideal world—what you want to see in the future. You can even include relationships that have been badly damaged or those that are nonexistent if you want them to be a part of your future.

5. How important is it for you to have a diversity of experiences? What do you want those experiences to be?

I love this question. It ignites me. Here is part of the answer I wrote when completing this exercise: "I want to be really poor and I want to be really rich. I want to live among many cultures, I want to try different foods, and listen to a variety of music, I want to play an instrument and speak a new language and swim in every ocean on the planet, and teach. I want to feel free, I want to build a house, start a company, bungee jump, read everything, climb a big mountain, see and make beautiful art, travel to every continent, discover something that helps others live better quality lives, start a society with great minds (like Ben Franklin did), be a mom, be a grandmother."

I have a long, long list of experiences I want to have before leaving the world. Making those experiences become a reality is a huge priority for me and directs a lot of my life decisions. For me, living a good life is living a full life. Listing out the experiences you want to have will give you clarity on how to start living your full life.

6. How do you want to impact the people you know? How do you want to impact the people you don't know at all?

This question focuses specifically on the impact you have on individuals, both people you know and strangers. Answers can be as vague as "I want to make children feel safe," or as specific as "I want to build a school in African countries so children in those regions can have a space to feel safe in." It can also be something simple like you want to make your friends feel heard.

7. How do you want to impact future generations?

This is similar to the legacy question but can be interpreted more broadly because impact doesn't have to be something tangible you leave behind, nor does it necessarily have to do with you personally. Your answer can be something as simple as "I want to leave the world a better place by focusing on reducing carbon emissions."

This answers to your Clarity Guide questions comprise your vision framework—the stilts on which everything else is built. Inherently, your answers will be a true reflection of you and what you value. When attempting to establish values, many methods try to get you to select words that represent what you value most—like "integrity" or "family." But I find these methods don't get to the core of what values really mean. Values are action based, and cannot be defined in one word. This Clarity Guide will unearth your values by naturally bringing to the surface the things that are most vital to you and the type of actions you want to take to represent those unique values in your life. When you re-read your answers, they should be deeply personal, they should trigger emotions, they should make you feel more like yourself than ever before. When you reread them, you should say, "This feels right. This is who I am."

If you are having trouble deciding whether to include certain things or how to answer these questions, remember that you do not want to limit yourself by size; there is nothing too small or too big to include. There's no "right amount" you need to write either; there's no "too much" or "too little." The only rule that should help you decide what to include is how important the answer is to you. How much does your answer affect your heart? If it has a significant impact, then you want to include it.

This exercise can be emotionally draining. That's normal. And, if you have never thought about these things before, that is okay. It is often true that we intentionally avoid thinking about these types of things because it is difficult. We might also avoid thinking about these topics because it is so far into the future that we don't think it matters. Or, these topics may be hard for us to think about because we haven't met our own expectations in these areas yet and that makes us sad. Those feelings—the ones of anxiety (what do I do next), disappointment (I haven't achieved what I wanted), and regret (how did my life go by so quickly)—are totally natural, normal, common, and expected. Don't let them stop you, let them drive you. If you experience these feelings, know that they're a part of the process—a necessary part. As I said before, this process is going to get harder before it gets better. But the better is absolutely, without a doubt, worth it, and it is the next step to achieving the life of your dreams.

You have a done an amazing job so far, and now, we are on to the fun part!

The next step in defining clarity is to start imagining what type of person you want to be. This will include visualizing the new you in different types of situations. The purpose of this visualization is to gain clarity from the inside out and make this person more than a vision. So, this next part is less about designing the direction of your life and more about the personality you will bring with you in the direction you head. It is part of gaining clarity on the type of person you will be spending the most time with (yourself). It is also the step that will allow you to get through difficult times easier than ever before. After this next exercise, you will likely find yourself with a renewed sense of self-confidence, stability, resilience, and inner-knowing.

This is how it works: imagine that ideal version of yourself—the one that's wise, calm, controlled, brilliant, inspiring, kind, selfless, and does everything perfectly. Of course, no perfect human exists, but that shouldn't stop us from creating these ideal versions of ourselves in our mind. Usually, our ideal selves are visions of a "future self," the version that finally gets it together—one day.

But here's the secret: today is actually that day. We are going to make this future self your new reality right now.

If you don't already imagine your future self, you can start here: imagine someone you admire. What do you admire about them? You can use that vision as a springboard to get you started on this next exercise.

At the end of this exercise, I always feel more grounded, more in touch with my true self, and less stressed. This exercise should make you feel good. It should flow and be easy. It should be energizing. If it isn't, I encourage you to stop, take a break, and try again another day.

Exercise 5: Creating the Ideal You

It is critical to write all your answers down because there is something transformative about putting your thoughts on paper. If you aren't one for words you can create a visual representation of this exercise—similar to a vision board, you can use pictures to answer each of the questions.

Let nothing stop you from defining the ultimate you, your way. You do not want any of your negative assumptions to creep in here and stop you from bringing to life the YOU of your dreams. This is why we addressed negative assumptions earlier in the book. When creating the ideal you, you are starting from scratch and you don't have to keep anything if you don't like it. You have already gained the tools to move past negative assumptions, cope with triggers, and build your ideal life without anything holding you back.

Part I: Answer the questions below as if you suddenly WERE the ideal version of yourself. These are just examples to get you started in painting a picture, you can add, skip or change any question you want.

- How do I handle difficult emotions?
- How do I present myself to the world? (Bubbly, calm, confident, quiet, outspoken, etc.)
- How do I look? What type of clothes do I wear? How do I style my hair? Where do I shop?
- How do I care for myself?
- How do I handle tragedy?
- How do I handle loss/failure/rejection?
- How do I relate to other people?
- What are my relationships like?
- What is my family like?
- How do I walk? Is my posture tall? Do I walk fast or slow?
- How do I talk? (Fast, slow, clear?)
- How do I communicate? Sophisticated, casual?
- Am I open minded?
- Am I outgoing?
- Am I confident?
- What hobbies do I have?
- How do I challenge myself?
- What is my routine in the morning and at bedtime?
- What time do I wake up in the morning?
- Do I exercise?
- What does my bedroom look like?
- How do I wake up? (With the alarm or with the sunrise?)

- Where do I live? What does my home look like? Do I live in the city? The suburbs?

- Do I have a vehicle? If so, what type of vehicle do I drive?

- How often do I see my friends?

- What do I do when I get sad?

- How do I act when I get sick?

- What happens when I am scared/anxious or nervous? Do I show it?

- Am I graceful?

- Do I go on adventures? Travel?

- How much of myself do I share with strangers? With friends? With family?

- What type of books do I read?

- What type of food do I eat?

- Do I have a job? If so, what is it?

- Is my house organized and clean? Do I care?

- Do I have pets?

- What climate do I live in?

- Can I cook? Play tennis? Play Chess? Speak other languages? Paint?

- How happy am I?

- Do I give to charity?

- What causes am I passionate about and how do I contribute to them?

Now we are going to take this new, ideal person and put that person in a variety of real and imagined situations. Some of these situations will have already happened and might represent instances in which you wish you would have acted differently. Some of these situations will be imaginary and some may be events that occur in the future. You are going to ask yourself, "How would the ideal version of myself act?" This helps crystallize the new you and give them life.

Here are some questions that will help further define the ideal you and allow you to practice facing different challenges.

Part II: Putting the new "you" into practice.

How would the ideal version of myself act if I time traveled back to a specific moment (have the moment in mind) in which I:

- Was rejected?
- Treated badly by a friend or partner?
- Got really, really angry?
- Was betrayed?

Using genuine moments in your life allows you to exercise the qualities of the ideal version of yourself in concrete situations. No other technique provides you with that opportunity. You can choose any past scenarios of significance to you but we don't want to linger and obsess here. The purpose is not to harp on changing an outcome, just to briefly note how you would have acted differently if you had been the new you.

Now we'll project the ideal you into the future. Part of the goal here is to realize, once you are your ideal you, there is nothing to dread or fear in life. This will open up more opportunities, generate action, and often will cultivate positivity and happiness. Don't be surprised if others start noticing a big change in you.

There are countless questions you can ask to project the ideal you into the future. I encourage you to use the ones provided here as inspiration and then add in your own. When you answer these questions, try to ensure you are in a neutral mindset. Don't sit down to answer these questions after a big fight or a promotion at work. Try to find an average day where you are clear-headed. This will help eliminate any temporary biases that could influence your answers.

Find a quiet space where you have time to reflect. I usually have to come back to these questions once a week for a month or so in order to finish painting the total picture of this vision. Sometimes, answering one question gives me a new perspective on other questions and I realize I want to change my answer or go deeper. That is all okay and an important part of the process.

Here is an example of a personal question I asked myself: Would I be nervous speaking in front of a hundred people, a thousand people? (The ideal me has NO fear. The current me is still working on this, but this exercise has helped tremendously.)

Sample Questions:

- What type of progress would the ideal version of myself make today in achieving my dreams?

- How would I handle stress, overwhelm or fatigue today if I was the "future" me?

- What would a day with the ideal me look like? What would I have accomplished?

- How would I handle separation from those I love? (Children, parents?)

- How would I channel strong emotions? (Writing, poetry, exercise, hobbies?)

- How do I want to age?

- What do I do in retirement?

- Do I mentor others? How? In what way?

- How do I continue to learn?

Asking yourself how the ideal version of yourself would act and then following through on those actions actually makes you the ideal version of yourself today, bit by bit. The more you do it, the more you become that person. It is almost magical.

As you become the ideal you, you will gain confidence to put yourself in more situations that allow you to hone the experience you want to gain. Over time, you start to realize the person you are trying to become has arrived. I sincerely hope this for each and every one of you reading this book. I know it is possible, and I cannot wait for you to join me on this life-long journey.

It's time to congratulate yourself. Deep self-reflection is uncommon, and it is uncommon because it is challenging. You have been driven and courageous enough to meet that challenge. That is an enormous accomplishment.

PART II
THE TRANSFORMATION

CHAPTER 6

ACTION

The next step is action. Action is the difference between living the life you want to live and living the life you are living now. In this next section, we take the new, improved you and we start integrating secret techniques, strategies, and tools to make your dreams reality.

As the passage of time allowed me to reflect upon my aspirations, I began to realize that I had been waiting for some external catalyst to bring my dreams to fruition. Maybe I was waiting to get even older, maybe I was waiting to make more money. I'm not sure. But I was waiting for something "out there." Then, as the years went by and kept on coming— it dawned on me that nothing big was going to come along and change things FOR me. I was the impetus for change and if I had any chance of achieving my most desired outcomes, it became evident that it would take decisive action, rather than hope and expectation, for my dreams to become reality.

Most people believe this myth: taking real, transformative action means huge, scary steps or giant leaps into high-risk scenarios. I often hear, "I cannot afford to," "I don't have the time," or "I don't have the motivation to do that right now." In reality, action does not necessarily mean big steps. It can mean small baby steps moving in the general direction toward where you want to end up.

The big secret is that you have to keep taking those baby steps, day after day after day. Action is the bridge between the now and your future vision. You did all the hard work, now you just have to take that next step of putting one foot in front of the other, and repeat.

For example, if you have always imagined yourself as someone who was very put together but, for some reason, you never seem to have enough time to get ready in the morning because you are always rushed, make a promise to yourself you will wake up fifteen minutes early so that you can start stepping into that vision. If you think a change like this is petty or insignificant, start doing it daily, and you will see its incredible power. Some of the changes you make at first might seem insignificant, but they aren't because they represent the ideal you coming to life. These small steps pave the way for the larger, more significant changes to become your permanent reality.

It is imperative that you create an environment that allows the best parts of yourself to be consistently expressed. For example, I bought myself a pair of expensive silk pajamas because the future version of myself was wearing a pair of silk pajamas to bed with matching slippers and a pillowcase. I don't know why this was part of my vision, but it was. Now, whenever I put on those luxurious pajamas, I feel like I am that person— my ideal self. That small step represents a bigger change for me, in me.

Don't write off the small changes because they seem insignificant; they are the beginning of a big transformation. It is the small steps that pave the way. For example, if you imagined yourself as a New York Times best-selling author, start a short blog, write a short story, and publish it—just for fun—and start stepping into that reality. These small steps might seem silly at first, but they have changed my life and they will change yours as well.

Once I started to physically and emotionally embody my ideal self, everything changed. It was a profound experience, and I have seen it work for countless others as well. This embodiment also includes changing your thoughts. Whenever I feel lost or intimidated now, I immediately ask my ideal self what would I do or think in that moment? I ask myself how do I want to look back and see that I handled this? As you start embodying your new life, you will start noticing obstacles disintegrate (did they ever really exist in the first place?), ideas emerging, and people offering you opportunities you never knew were possible.

I believe the most difficult challenges are the ones we create for ourselves in our mind. I see living a life of mediocrity, but always feeling disappointed in it, as far more challenging than working an eighty-hour work week in the direction of your dreams. If you don't know what to do or how to do it, start making the small changes to become your "ideal self" and you will see more doors open and more opportunities arise, you will find mentors, and you will see new ideas emerge. Better yet, I bet you that your newfound opportunities will end up matching up to your vision framework from your answers in the Clarity Guide. Once you define who you want to be, and then you become that person, everything starts to shift in the direction of the life you want.

A note on disappointment and expectations: I don't want anyone reading this book to think this process is automatic and linear. You will have many days of being your "old self" in between small spurts of becoming your "ideal self." That is completely normal. The only thing that matters is that you try again the next day, particularly after setbacks. While it is almost certain you will face obstacles in becoming your ideal self, the victory is getting closer to that vision with each passing day.

Don't be surprised if things throw you off track, like getting sick or injured, your car breaking down, a big work project that saps all of your energy, or kids (the biggest derailer of all plans), or bigger things, like losing your job or going through a divorce. Becoming your ideal self isn't about being perfect, it's about getting closer to being the person you want to be when you die. That person needs to deal with all of the things that life throws at you too, and sometimes becoming your ideal self is more about how you deal with the things that throw you off track then it is about being on track in the first place.

Now that we've talked about becoming the person you want to be, let's talk about some strategies to live life on your terms when things inevitably don't go your way.

CHAPTER 7

WHERE THERE'S A WILL,
THERE'S A WAY

We already spoke about creating your ideal life, now we are going to learn what to do when life tells you NO despite your best efforts.

There is always a way. No is never your last answer. When someone tells you no, you immediately know that one (or both) of these things isn't strong enough . . . yet:

1. Your leverage, or

2. Your value proposition.

I will show you how to strengthen both your leverage and your unique value proposition with strategies that will make it possible for you to get what you desire a majority of the time.

Keep in mind, these strategies work whether or not you apply them ethically. I am sharing these techniques with the assumption that my readers will, of course, always use them responsibly. With that said, here is the guide to getting what you want, fast.

What are the most important skills you need in order to achieve your vision?

I am not going to talk about the basics: showing up, dressing nice, being prepared, organized, emotionally intelligent, and reliable—those are obvious. Anyone who is reading this book has already mastered those skills and more. This is about the skills that are often hidden, but always used by the most powerful people in the world. These are the secret strategies that will take you to the next level.

The first skill is the ability to think outside the box, but specifically in getting to what you want, against all odds. You will almost never go from A to B on the things that really matter. It will be A first, then staying at A, arriving at A again, suddenly finding yourself at C, then back to B, etc. Most people try to go from A to B directly and then give up at the first sign of an obstacle. But I go in expecting and preparing for obstacles. I spend time planning and anticipating the obstacles and figuring out, early on, how to use those obstacles to MY advantage.

Early on in my career, in one of my jobs, I decided I wanted to be promoted to a director level position. At that point I was a senior project manager. It didn't intimidate me one bit that my company's traditional career trajectory was as follows: project manager, senior project manager, supervisor, manager, then director (with two years at each step, on average). We can never let obscurely set rules stop us from achieving what we know we are ready for and capable of. I went and asked my boss for the promotion—I came in with a full proposal and reasons why I should get the new role. He said . . . drumroll . . . no. I was told that everyone had to follow a specific, organization-wide career trajectory. But guess what? I wasn't everyone, and neither are you. He told me the good ole (and expected) responses: "If we did this for you, we would have to do this for everyone else," "we have to follow company policy," etc. I thought to myself, "When other employees can bring the type of value I am offering then they should be promoted too."

So, I waited a few more months, took on some big projects, showing I was doing work equivalent to others at the director level, collected even more evidence of my readiness and capabilities, and tried again asking for the director role. (This is an example of taking the obvious route and trying to go from A to B, again). My boss said no, again. Frustrated, I started to think that I wasn't going to achieve my goal. This is where most people stop—but I knew that I wasn't going to take no for an answer. However, I also knew what I was doing just wasn't working. I suddenly realized I needed step back and look at first principles. I wasn't pushing on the right levers, and I wasn't taking my own advice.

If you aren't getting what you want, you either:

1. Don't have enough leverage, or

2. Don't have a strong enough value proposition.

I knew I had a strong value proposition, but continuing to force that angle wasn't going to give me new results. What I was missing was... leverage! So, I went to a company similar to the company I was working for and got an offer for a director title (they hired me on the spot because I had a high value proposition), they offered me a salary approximately forty percent higher than current earnings. Suddenly (and I mean within twenty-four hours) I was promoted to director at the company I was currently working at with a much larger salary than if I had been promoted without that leverage. In fact, my leverage was so strong I only needed to drop hints about the offer and new salary for them to quickly realize that by adhering to their arbitrary promotion hierarchy they were about to lose me and the value I brought to their company. In fact, I never even had to ask for the director role—they just gave it to me. THAT is what good leverage can do for you.

By now you know that this example is not about a better title or money, it is about understanding how to get what you want in countless scenarios in life and what levers to pull and push in almost any situation. This is a winning formula and it has never once failed me. Again, the two levers you always want to question if things aren't going your way are your value proposition and your leverage. If you have both, you will very rarely (if ever) lose out on what you want. You can use these two levers to your advantage, but you must make sure that both your value and your leverage are genuine.

I am not talking about taking a shortcut, or getting more for nothing. This is about clearly defining your worth based on real value that only you can create, showing that value, and then making what you want happen despite everything you have going against you.

A Word on Negotiation

Much wiser men and women than I have written comprehensive books on negotiation, so I am not going to get deep into that here (one of my favorite books is *Never Split the Difference* by Chris Voss—if you read anything, read this). But, I will say that studying negotiation, and practicing negotiation, is a skill that will benefit you for the rest of your life. A skilled negotiator can bend luck and fate to their will.

Creating Your Most Powerful Value Proposition

Most people crave both financial stability and flexibility, but most people also think those two are mutually exclusive in the real world. I am here to tell you, that isn't true. Not one bit true, and anyone who thinks you can't have both is not thinking creatively enough. The solution is deceptively simple. The way to design your schedule (and life), on your terms, is to simply have no other acceptable option. Of course, this comes with being very clear on how you are going to provide extraordinary contributions and value to the point where you can make such an impact for an individual or an organization that they won't mind if you work one hour a week...from outer space. How do you do that? A powerful value proposition.

Now, I am not recommending you work one hour a week, from space, but I am recommending that you cultivate an incredibly strong value proposition to justify your demands. This value proposition you create will work with an employer, a client, a patient, an investor, or anyone else that you want to buy into YOU (although I can't claim it works on toddlers, if only).

Exercise 6: The Value Proposition

Imagine if you had a few sentences, that when spoken or written could change your life. Imagine these sentences could help get you more promotions, better jobs, higher pay, more success, and growth. In this chapter, you are going to create those sentences. The sentences are called a value proposition.

To create an amazing and successful value proposition, there are four foundational questions you want to ask. These questions bring out the four components of a winning value proposition: uniqueness, motivation, leverage, and vision.

Fill out these questions to the best of your ability and then practice explaining your answers, again and again—in front of a mirror, for friends and family, online—until it seems natural and flows out of you, like saying your own name.

1. What can you and only you contribute to your industry, niche, area of expertise?

2. What is it about what you are contributing that is going to drive you to be the BEST at it?

3. What will happen if they (employers or customers) lose you?

4. How can you not only achieve your/their goals, but create a new, better vision for them/yourself/your customers?

If you are thinking that you can't create such a value proposition easily, I am here to tell you that yes, you absolutely can, and I will help you get there.

Start building your value proposition by using this question guide:

1. What is one thing you do or something unique you have done that makes you stand out, apart from others? *Uniqueness*

2. What inspired you to go into the field/business/area you are in? (Including if you're a stay-at-home parent.) *Your motivation.*

For example, did someone in your family get sick, and the experience made you want to go into healthcare? Did your battle with poverty make you want to help others manage their money? Did your passion for math in grade school drive you into analytics? Did your love of kids and of your childhood make you want to be a full-time caretaker?

These are your drivers, your motivators, and they give you an edge. They should always be integrated into your value proposition.

3. If you aren't easily replaced, why?

If you are easily replaced, then you need to work on differentiating your skill set. You want what you are doing to have a difficult barrier to entry, either because of skill, training, education, or inventiveness. *This will define your leverage.*

4. Are the goals you are trying to achieve either for yourself or on behalf of a larger unit, the right goals? Why are those goals in place? What is the overall vision and how can you contribute to or improve it? *Vision*

Thinking ahead, seeing the bigger picture—improving, revitalizing or rewriting the vision—will take you to the next level.

I hope this helps you realize that you CAN make a strong value proposition, and with it in your back pocket, you will be absolutely unstoppable.

CHAPTER 8

BE A SUPERSTAR

Whether we work for someone else, own a business, or do anything else in this world, it's of utmost importance to present your value to the world and know how to increase it. So, how do you accomplish that? By learning not only the raw skill, but the essential presentation of that skill as well.

Through my work, I have observed thousands of people. There are four types of people I notice most:

1. the individual who is really good at what they do but who doesn't know how to sell their value,

2. the person who isn't that good but knows how to play the game and pretend (talking about doing without doing),

3. the individual who can produce amazing work and showcase their talent to others (introducing the star), and finally

4. the person that is really good at what they do, can communicate the value of their work, AND can effectively communicate how their potential will increase in value exponentially over time (the superstar).

This concept of super stardom can apply to anyone—those who service clients, own a small business, want to start a business, work with investors or invests, or anyone else out there producing outcomes of value in one way or another.

Be a superstar. Sure, the stars move ahead. But the superstars will move ahead at lightning speed while the rest rarely reach their potential because they cannot sell themselves or their work in a way that reaches and impacts others.

Let's look at the applicable truths of what defines a superstar.

The Superstar

Superstars have a special talent. They can see the larger picture. They have the ability to look at a project, initiative, or idea and ask where and how it fits in the overall plan. This comprehensive perspective usually lends itself to creating visions, and those who have visions tend to become leaders. Superstars can easily zoom their perspective in and out for any situation. They can look at problems, challenges, and obstacles from different angles. As a result, they are able to anticipate needs which helps them to produce optimal outcomes, professionally and personally. Superstars increase value simply by virtue of how they operate, making them invaluable.

Whenever I come across a superstar, it's immediately obvious—they have a mix of perspective, ambition, talent, emotional intelligence, and salesmanship. It is an unmistakable combination. When I see one, I note it. Lo and behold, a few years later they have accomplished more than those twice their age. The superstar is unstoppable because they have a little bit of all of the qualities required to create a positive explosion that shoots them to the top of any business, project, or initiative.

Don't feel too badly for the stars. They do well, but they also tend to stagnate, unable to know where to go next, lacking the ability to showcase their past accomplishments and future potential. The stars often end up in one position for a long time, they are less likely to take risks, and they are consistent, but rarely surprise you. The world needs stars, but this book was written specifically to unearth more superstars—those of you who want to change the world and will stop at nothing until you do.

I believe that most of the superstar qualities are inherited, not learned, but it is also true that you can inherit these qualities, exhibit them in childhood or early adulthood, and then lose them. You could also have not exhibited them in childhood and find them in adulthood for the first time, but more often than not, you will see these qualities early on, and something or someone extinguished them.

Superstars usually (although there are always exceptions) aren't made, they are born. Knowing this helps you recognize if you might be a superstar. Do you remember having superstar qualities as a child? It is not something you usually forget. If you did have them, when? If they dissipated, why? Failure, hardships, illnesses, trauma, and more can stifle superstar qualities. But guess what? If you had them once, they're still there. It's time to let your superstar re-emerge.

In the next three chapters, we are going to learn my secret recipe for incredible direction, focus, and productivity—required characteristics for any superstar. Developing these secrets took me decades of trial and error. They are the answer to the question you will inevitably get, "How do you do it all?", and I cannot wait for my secrets to become your own.

CHAPTER 9

THE ULTIMATE TO-DO LIST

Making the right to-do list impacts success, satisfaction, and well-being. In this chapter, you will learn how to create a to-do list that will allow you to accomplish the things you never thought were possible.

To start, write down everything you want to accomplish in one day. Yep, just one single day. No item is too small or too large. You can include anything that you want, from washing your car to starting a business, walking your dog, or making dinner.

There is no need to be fancy. Here is an example illustrating the list's simplicity:

- Wash Car
- Run 2 miles on treadmill
- Make dentist Apt
- Kids Laundry
- Pack for Palm Springs
- Write 2 chapters of book
- 2pm meeting

- Return package at FedEx
- Prep for dinner at 5pm

The second step is to split these items into the following two categories: items that require little energy and items that require high energy. Keep in mind that low and high energy items look different for everyone. For me, working out is actually a low energy item because I like to do it and it gives me a break from work. A high energy item for me would be something that requires a lot of creative thought and brainpower. My high energy items usually include things I don't necessarily enjoy doing, while the things I enjoy usually require less energy and can even reinvigorate me.

You will, on some days, inevitably notice a group of neutral items on your to-do list that don't fall into high or low energy categories. That's okay. These are usually the items you just have to get done each day and the items for which you don't have much flexibility (like mandatory meetings or doctors' appointments at specific times, for example). It is your choice whether or not to include these neutral items in your final list. Sometimes I just leave them to the side in a category tagged "other." It helps me to keep them in view so I can get a full picture of the layout of my day.

If you are in a situation with little flexibility to choose when to complete certain activities during your day—for example, you have to be on the phone most of the day for work—then this high/low energy to-do list should be applied during the hours when you do have some flexibility, such as before or after work. The point of this list is energy management. You want to make sure you have some high and low energy item categorization to manage your energy when you get the opportunity to do so. The goal is to be prepared to spend your time as powerfully as possible.

The overall purpose with this to-do list is to make progress on the big picture items that really matter to you. Generally, we all have some wherewithal to organize our day, most days. This organization strategy ensures that the most impactful things get done.

An average to-do list for me might look something like this:

High Energy Items	Low Energy Items
Writing 3 chapters in my book	Going for a 30-minute run
Reviewing tax documents	Shopping for kids back to school items
PowerPoint presentation	Baking fresh bread
Upgrading public health website	Organizing closet
Spending time with my parents	
Other	
Meetings (10 a.m., 2 p.m., 3 p.m., 5 p.m.)	
Dentist Appointment (9 a.m.)	

My daily to-do list might also include items that help me improve in areas where I am striving to be better (like spending more quality time with my kids), and investing in activities that make me feel happy (going to lunch with a friend).

Additionally, I always put my health goals as the first items on the list (e.g., drink smoothie, run 2 miles). I also try to put one thing on the list each day that makes me uncomfortable and that challenges me (this could be something physical, like doing a hard workout, or something emotionally challenging, like volunteering with sick patients). Of course, not all of these items will make it on the daily to-do list depending on what else I have going on that week.

Once the list is split into high/low energy and "other," I put an asterisk next to one to four items on the list (in either category) that I want to accomplish above all else. This helps me prioritize. The prioritized items should be the ones that help you achieve your big picture, long-term goals. For example, writing my dissertation helped me achieve my overall goals, while doing the dishes just kept things going. So, for example, I would not highlight doing the dishes as a priority (even if I really needed to get them washed). Low energy items can be priority items too. You want to make sure they get done, but they don't necessarily need to be done during high energy times.

Here is another to-do list example with my starred priority items:

High Energy Items	Low Energy Items
*Writing 3 chapters in my book	*Going for a 30-minute run
Reviewing tax documents	Shopping for kids' back to school items
*PowerPoint presentation	Baking fresh bread
Upgrading public health website	Organizing closet
*Spending time with my parents	
Other	
Meetings (10 a.m., 2 p.m., 3 p.m., 5 p.m.)	
Dentist Appointment	

The top priority is to accomplish the starred items. However, if something interferes with your ability to complete your starred items, it's very important to give yourself grace and patience and then get back to those priority items the following day. Usually, I'm able to finish my prioritized items because this to-do list helps me focus and hone in on what's important. For example, if my two priority items for the day are working out and finishing one chapter of my book, then I know where I am going to be focusing the energy and time I have for that day when I have the choice.

If I need a break or get tired before my high energy items are complete, I switch over to some low energy items (priority first). That is the beauty of the low energy items—they give your mind and/or body a needed break but still allow you to be productive and feel accomplished at the end of the day while meeting your goals. It is the best of both worlds.

Regardless of what else I decide to accomplish on any given day, I will have completed the things most important to me—the things that drive my life in the right direction. At first, this might seem like a lot of planning just to get through your day, but if you're not intentional about what you do, then the days, weeks, and years will quickly pass you by. This method guarantees intentionality, and all but ensures you make progress in achieving the goals in your Clarity Guide.

Once you get used to it, creating this to-do list usually doesn't take more than one minute. I create mine on my iPhone Notes app right before I get into bed. Once the list is written, I can sleep better knowing my time will be spent the following day completing the things that will move my life forward.

In the following pages, we will expand on how exactly to put this to-do list into practice in a way that will make you more productive than you have ever been. Not only will you be focusing on the right things, but you will be completing them in a fraction of the time, consistently. These are the habits that really do turn a pipe dream into reality.

A to-do list template can be found in the downloadable workbook which you can access for free at www.drjendunphy.com/books.

CHAPTER 10

ENERGY

In this chapter, you will learn exactly how to organize your day around your energy levels—not around time, meetings, or people. This means getting to know your energy patterns.

Becoming aware of my own energy patterns has allowed me to pinpoint when I perform best, when I'm at my most creative, and when I need to do something mindless. Through energy charting (explained below), I have found that I am almost always a morning person—not that I like to wake up early, but in the morning when I do wake up, I am my most creative and focused self. This means I schedule my most important work in the morning. I never take important conversations between 2 to 4 p.m. if I can avoid it, because that's when I experience my energy slump. I perk up around 4 p.m. again and have fairly high energy until 11 p.m. I plan every day accordingly, and with tremendous results.

In the next exercise, I am going to show you how you can reveal your personal energy patterns by creating your own energy profile. Then, I will show you how to use that energy profile in order to become the most productive you have ever been.

Exercise 7: Energy Charting

Energy charting will take a minimum of two weeks. An energy charting template can be found in the downloadable workbook which you can access for free at www.drjendunphy.com/books.

First, split each day into two-hour blocks (see chart below): 7-9, 9-11, 11-1, 1-3, 3-5, 5-7, 7-9, 9-11, 11-1.

Then, rate your energy levels (1 (lowest energy) to 5 (highest energy) in each of those blocks in which you are awake, every day, for a minimum of two weeks. The longer you are able to chart, the more likely the information you collect will represent your true energy profile. I recommend re-doing this exercise at least once a year, or any time you introduce new stressors or big changes into your life (moving, deaths, births, new jobs, new partner, etc.). Life stressors, both positive and negative, can make huge impacts on our energy patterns.

You will likely find interesting results when you chart your energy levels. Most people are surprised when they take the time and discipline to engage in this energy charting activity.

You know that you have successfully completed this exercise when you begin to see consistent patterns in your energy levels. This is your energy profile. You will see, on average, when your energy peaks, and when it falls—often you will have little dips and little peaks that you never noticed before. If you decide to chart for a longer period of time, you may also find weekly and monthly patterns as well. However, I tend to use my daily energy profile to drive my productivity because I find that it is the most reliable. This is some of the most valuable information you can gather and it will drive your ability to become the best, most productive version of yourself.

We do not want to bend our energy to our work; we want to bend our work to our energy. If you can master this, you will be significantly more productive, less frustrated, and experience less burnout.

My energy profile, on average, looks like this:

Time	Energy Score
7-9 a.m.	4
9-11 a.m.	5
11-1 p.m.	3
1-3 p.m.	1
3-5 p.m.	3
5-7 p.m.	3
7-9 p.m.	3
9-11 p.m.	3

Jen's Energy Profile (average day)

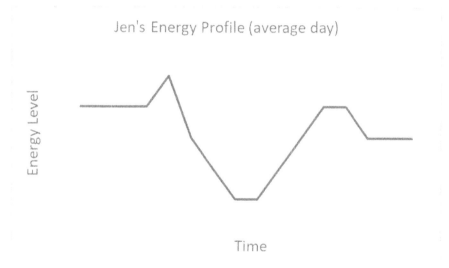

As you can see, my energy peak is in the morning. Then, I have a major afternoon slump, usually between 1 and 3 p.m., after which my energy starts to rise again into the evening, and then drops around the time I go to bed. This information drives my productivity. We usually only have about two to three hours in our highest productivity state, so it's vital that we don't squander those hours completing lower value tasks.

Next, let's talk about how to combine your energy data with your to-do list so that you can make the most of your high and low energy periods.

Take a look at your to-do list and select the items that are the hardest to accomplish. These are the items that take the most focus and energy and they should be under the high energy heading of your to-do list. These items are also usually the ones that you would tend to procrastinate the most on, and that require your mind to focus for long periods of time without the dopamine-boosting *ding* of cell phone notifications.

These tasks are your **big-ticket priority (starred) items** that will help you accomplish your dreams, and they should ideally be matched with your highest energy/focus periods because that's when you will be able to focus most effectively.

The items in your neutral or low energy categories will then be matched with the biggest dip of energy in your day. These items can be reserved for low energy times when you will inevitably be less productive in accomplishing more complex tasks.

How to find your high-value tasks

Identifying your high-value tasks is not always obvious, especially when you have a very busy daily to-do list. It can be easy, yet detrimental to your BIG goals, to conflate busyness with productivity. Busyness is like running in place as fast as you can—you are working hard but you aren't going anywhere. That is why identifying which tasks should be flagged as high-priority is crucial. Sometimes it is obvious, like folding laundry versus working on a high-visibility work presentation. But sometimes, it is not as clear. For example, putting together a business plan for a new business you have been thinking about starting versus answering emails. This is where people get stuck and end up using their most valuable time periods engaged in lower-value tasks. Sure, e-mails need answering, but sitting down and putting together that business plan is what is going to move you forward. The reason some people get confused is that they think answering e-mails will only take a few minutes, so they want to "get it out of the way." This is the kiss of death for deep productivity. It is an avoidance tactic—another way to put off the big, complex, high-value project. Don't let it trap you. Imagine what you could accomplish if all the "it will just take a few minutes" moments were strung together and invested in a high-value project.

If you are having a hard time deciding which tasks should be high-value, you are not alone. Fortunately, there a few tell-tall signs that can help you differentiate between high-value tasks and tasks. Most of us have unique indicators that can help us physically and emotionally distinguish important tasks from lower-value tasks. If your mind doesn't know, often your body does.

Personally, when a task is high-value and intense, I find myself wanting to pick up my phone and scroll so that my brain can "rest." I also find myself wanting to squirm (which is why I try and exercise first), and I even find myself thinking of all the other things I have to do instead of the high-value task (organize my fridge, do the dishes, call an old friend, answer emails, etc.). But, since I am aware of my avoidance patterns, I can recognize them and say, "Oh, this is just how I act when I am engaging in a challenging task and I know it is time for me to sit in the discomfort and focus on this."

Think about what projects on your list would make you feel disappointed or anxious if you didn't accomplish them. I tend to use my anxiety as fuel; if I am anxious about a project not getting done, that usually signifies both its difficulty and, simultaneously, its importance. I use that anxiety or frustration as a guidepost to let me know that I am moving in the right direction in categorizing that task as a high-priority item.

It is not always true that high-value tasks are uncomfortable. If you can get into a state of flow (a creative space where you don't even notice time passing), then completing the task will be easier. However, if you can easily enter a state of flow with your high-value tasks then they should be listed under the "low-energy" category since they do not require as much discipline and energy to complete.

Another way to decide if a task is high-value or not is to imagine how proud of yourself you would feel if you accomplished it to the best of your ability. If the task is both high-value and difficult, you will feel incredibly proud. That's another signal that the task should be recognized as a high-priority item.

If you can match your high-energy times with your high-value/priority items, then you will succeed. Your high-energy times are critical periods of time when the real work gets done, and it is what distinguishes the good from the great, and the average from the extraordinary.

If you find yourself wanting to pick up your phone excessively, it may simply mean your brain is ready for a break. Many people cannot concentrate for longer than ninety minutes at a time. That is perfectly normal and okay!

When you start to feel unfocused in your work, you can set a dedicated time to take a break. During that break, I would not recommend zoning out (usually via the phone) but instead engaging in a restorative activity, such as a walk, meditation, or a catch-up with a good friend. When you are not on a dedicated break, it is often useful to place your phone out of reach or in another room. If you find yourself only able to focus for twenty minutes at a time, that is okay too. Your ability to focus is like any other skill: it needs to be practiced and honed. I remember after I wrote my dissertation, I was able to focus for more than six hours at a time. A year (and a baby) later, that came down to only thirty minutes!

In the next chapter, we'll discover the last piece of the productivity puzzle, which enhances every strategy we have discussed and allows you to keep achieving and achieving until you reach your vision. These strategies are the key for transforming your vision into reality.

CHAPTER 11

THE MINIMUM SCHEDULE

This final scheduling strategy builds on the framework of the previous two strategies we just discussed—the high/low energy to-do list and the energy profile. Big goals and large projects must be broken up into chunks. In order to do this most effectively, I use what I call a "minimum schedule." The minimum schedule is simply the minimum amount of work/activities/physical exercise that you want to accomplish in one day. However, when using the minimum schedule, I always invite myself to accomplish more if I am in the mood (the only time I let my mood dictate my work is after my minimum schedule work is complete). Devising a schedule that focuses on a minimum number of activities motivates me so much that I usually end up finishing my project in half the time I would have without it!

The minimum schedule works like this: if I want to write a book, I will say the minimum activity to accomplish that goal is to write **ONE** chapter a day. If I do that, then I have accomplished my big task for the day! This task will be one that is starred under my high-energy to-do items. I will work on that one chapter during the high energy times indicated in my energy profile. After I finish a high priority task, I usually feel great. In fact, I often feel so good and motivated that I can't wait to keep going and accomplish more.

With a normal schedule, having a large goal makes you feel bad if you don't reach it, contributing to future inertia. On the other hand, a smaller goal makes you feel like you can and should stop once you complete that goal. By using the concept of completing "at least" a minimum amount of work, you will be propelled forward in a way that truly taps into our psychological needs for positive motivation. This motivation helps sustain our work, complete more work, and acts as a complement to the energy-based to-do list I described above.

Here is an example of the minimum schedule in action:

High-Energy:

Go for AT LEAST a 5-minute walk (this usually turns into a 30-minute walk)

*Finish AT LEAST 2,000 words of my book

*Finish AT LEAST one paragraph of my newsletter

Low-Energy:

*Work out AT LEAST 25 minutes (treadmill or pilates)

Read for AT LEAST 10 minutes

	Activity	Minimum Work
High-Energy	Take a walk	5 mins
	*Write book	2000 words
	*Newsletter	1 paragraph
Low-Energy	*Work out (treadmill)	25 minutes
	Read	10 minutes

I try to make the minimum amount of work in my minimum schedule reasonable enough to encourage me to start the task and combat inertia, but also significant enough to feel accomplished when complete.

It might seem like a lot of planning just to get a to-do list together, but it will get easier and faster over time. For example, I usually keep the same minimum time for many of my daily items; the time in which they are completed, as well as *when* they are completed, becomes a habit on autopilot. The results you see from doing this regularly will astound you and the lifelong habits you can build from using this method can change your life.

In order to determine your minimum schedule numbers (they can be pages/miles/steps/sales/or anything else that's quantifiable), think about the minimum number that, if completed five days of the week, would significantly drive you forward in accomplishing your goals. When you add up the minutes (or any quantifiable unit) for each project from your daily minimums, they should add up to something you are proud of, while simultaneously feeling like you could consistently keep working at that pace. The point of these numbers is not to start with something overly ambitious, but to start with something that will encourage you to continue the task consistently, day after day. An ambitious goal is just a bunch of smaller goals stitched together!

The minimum amount of time or work for each task is going to be different for everyone, but there are some guidelines I like to use. For physical activity, I find that **twenty-five minutes** is a great starting point. It is short enough where I never put it off, and regularly engaging in physical activity only makes me want to do it more. I usually end up doing more than twenty-five minutes, but knowing I only *have* to do twenty-five minutes to complete my daily goal encourages me to keep it up.

When looking at a project that requires you to focus, think about what amount of work is reasonable to complete in **ninety minutes** (the amount of time an average person can focus), then cut that work in half and make that your first completion goal. That gives you a really reasonable task to start with.

As you get into the habit of doing something (anything) every day (or five days a week), it becomes significantly easier to increase the time you spend doing it. Working on high-value tasks is like a muscle that needs to be trained. As your mind becomes accustomed to the new habit, you can slowly increase your minimums. It is important to be aware that as you increase the time in your minimum schedule, you don't want to reach too high a level of work where it becomes hard or stressful to complete every day. That is the exact opposite of what we are trying to accomplish. The beauty of this schedule is that it keeps you at a consistent pace. In my experience, consistency is much more valuable (and adds much more to your overall productivity and outcomes) than variable, larger chunks of work.

If you think this won't work for you, I challenge you to try a minimum schedule for one month and keep track of your progress. Add up your minimum schedule productivity for the month and compare it to the work you got done the month before. Most people are shocked to learn how much more they can get done by keeping this schedule day-after-day!

These strategies are for anyone who can see themselves benefiting from more productivity. This is also for people who struggle with completing large, overwhelming tasks and for those that are high-functioning procrastinators.

A high-functioning procrastinator is someone who always gets the work done but usually at the last minute. No one ever finds out how much this person procrastinates because they end up getting everything done before the deadline, keeping suspicions low. The issue with a functional procrastinator is that they usually have a lot of untapped potential. If you are one of these people, this schedule will help you access that potential. You should start noticing results almost immediately—especially in the way you feel about engaging in important projects that you normally procrastinate on or dread doing.

The key for the minimum schedule strategy to work is <u>consistency</u>, so don't expect the schedule to work *for* you—you have to show up and get started. But after you show up, the rest is gravy!

Together, these strategies will help you break negative patterns, accomplish what you once thought was impossible and turn your dreams into a physical reality.

CHAPTER 12

INSPIRATION

One of the most common excuses from people who want to do great things but just "can't" is that they think that they have to wait for inspiration to "hit" them one day in order to think of new ideas, start a business, write, paint, create, or even work out.

But the most successful people know that this notion is the opposite of the truth. Perseverance, not inspiration, breeds success. It is perseverance and consistency coupled with passion that create the inspiration, not the other way around.

Some people have waited half their lives for the inspiration to hit, for that million-dollar idea, for that motivation to write their book, start that small business, podcast, or blog. Most of the time, it never comes.

The best inspiration you can find is to get started. The productivity techniques you have learned in this book will help you master consistency and build up your focus, which will in turn allow you to finally find that inspiration you seek.

I always say that a mediocre *something* is better than an amazing nothing. You can improve upon your product later, if you want. But once you get started, sometimes you realize that creation in and of itself was the only inspiration you needed. This approach takes mental toughness, self-discipline, and mastery over your own (often lazy, in my case) mind.

Achieving mastery of mind is one of the main pillars of success. Mastery of mind means consistently doing things you don't feel like doing but which are in your best interest. The times I have been most frustrated, most overwhelmed, most intellectually burnt out were paradoxically the times I've also learned the most, grown the most, and made massive strides in achieving my greatest accomplishments. For me, the biggest telltale sign of success is if I am uncomfortable. Does my brain feel like it is going to explode because it's trying so hard to understand a concept? That is how I know I am getting somewhere.

Inspiration and motivation to do something unique and special is not something that just comes to most of us "one day." It is something you have to work hard for, and most of the time you won't "feel" like doing it; but it's in the doing it anyway that holds the power.

Of course, there are certain things you can do to increase the probability you will feel more motivated. Making sure your body is in peak condition is paramount. There is nothing worse than trying to focus and work when you are sick, nursing a hangover, exhausted, lethargic, in pain, too full, or emotionally drained. That is why it is imperative to prioritize my emotional, physical, and mental health over work. The reality though is that it is not ALWAYS possible to put yourself first.

My household was recently hit with the dreaded . . . preschool. Within the first week of my son attending school, my whole family came down with a respiratory virus. As I attempted to push forward in writing this book—on my fifth box of tissues, raw and peeling nose, nostril tampons in—I realized I was in exactly the type of situation where I would tell my readers to give themselves grace to rest and heal. So, I closed up my laptop and took a much-needed nap.

Unfortunately, that one cold turned into two colds back-to-back, and then three. Now, I was three weeks in, and three colds later (it turns out the preschoolers aren't the only ones needing to build their immunity). At this point, I had gained a few pounds from not working out, lost many hours of important work time, and was starting to feel like I was losing my motivation altogether.

Instead of spiraling into unproductivity, I used THIS book to help me get back on track (yes, really!). I started by implementing a new, gentler minimum schedule in which I cut my normal workout times and work times in half! The new minimum schedule took into account my new routine, obligations, and the resulting stress on my body.

In no time, I was back to achieving something that I felt proud of, every day. The new minimum schedule, although lighter, wasn't a set-back, it was an adjustment—one that took into account how my life was evolving.

You DON'T have to be perfect and you DON'T always have to increase your productivity week after week. Sometimes, expecting less of yourself actually helps you achieve more in the end. Had I kept trying to achieve my old minimum schedule, I would have found myself discouraged, wanting to give up altogether.

This book is meant to serve YOU. You are the master. It should enable you to follow a set of best-practices that allow you to do and be your best no matter what else is happening around you. It is a tool that can evolve with you as your life throws obstacle after obstacle in your face, which it will . . . *ACHOO!*

Your Calling

What if the problem is that you simply don't know what to do. If you aren't currently in your calling, you may feel a little off, a little anxious, a little like you aren't sure you are supposed to be spending time the way you are spending it. You know you have the fire burning inside of you to do something great, you KNOW you want to change the world, but maybe you don't know how or in what way. What if you want to do something amazing, but you just don't know what amazing thing to do?

Have you ever felt like this? This usually means you haven't quite found your calling yet—and I've been there.

Questions you might have include:

- I am interested in so many things, how will I ever decide which one to choose? How will I know if it's right?
- What if what I finally choose to do is a failure?
- What if I have never done something like this before? Who am I to try?
- What if I am not an expert—how will I ever compare?

First, you don't have to succeed—sometimes it's even better that you don't. If you read about the journeys of the founders of some of the most profitable companies of our time (called unicorns in Silicon Valley speak), you will see that these founders almost always have one thing in common—they fail before they succeed—often many times over. Don't look for the "perfect" project. It doesn't have to be your life's work. If you wait for perfection, if you wait for inspiration, all you end up doing is... waiting.

The One Question

One question, above all else, has gotten me further in my life in figuring out my own calling. When I answer this question, it puts everything into perspective and allows me to focus on how I want to spend my time.

The One Question is: If you found out tomorrow that your time here on earth was over, what would you be really disappointed about not having done in your life?

Whatever comes to your mind first, is usually the thing you need to do.

Sometimes your answer to this question might seem crazy, outlandish or impossible. Good! That means you ARE meant for greatness. And, sometimes you need to interpret the answer symbolically. For example, let's say you answered that you would be really disappointed that you didn't get to climb Mt Everest. For a few of you, it will mean that you should actually go climb Mt. Everest—but for most of you—it will mean that you need to do something in your life that makes you feel LIKE you climbed Mt. Everest. It could mean you need more intense challenges in your life, or that you want more physical adventure, or it could simply mean you want to attempt something really difficult and bold.

Depending on what your answer to this question is, you need to decide if its meaning is literal or symbolic. To figure that out, ask yourself a follow-up question:

What would it mean to me if I actually _____ (insert your answer to the One Question here)?

This second answer, and the feeling it evokes, is what you want from your calling.

Making small steps in the direction of your true calling should produce a sense of relief and a feeling of immense "rightness". You will know when you are on your path; it usually feels like you are being challenged to be your best-self in a way that makes you feel blissfully satisfied and also as if you are fulfilling a sense of duty. It is unmistakable. It feels like home. And, it means you are beginning to circle your calling.

I believe that we ALL have a calling. For some, life circumstances make it easier to connect with that calling sooner. For the rest of us, it takes work. I did not easily find my calling—it might even be the job of my lifetime, to get as close to it as I can.

I have many interests, I like to think big picture, and I have a variety of skills—this makes it really hard for me to find my ONE calling. If this sounds like you as well, don't worry. This usually means you need to broaden your definition of a calling. It may not be a specific job—instead it may be a category of problem you are able to solve better than others, or the way you can make people feel, or even a special way of communicating. Once you expand your definition of what a calling can mean, you will open up doors to a more inclusive definition of what your calling will look like for you, as a unique individual.

If you don't know what your calling is yet, that is more than okay. The self-exploration chapters of Awareness and Clarity will help you start to figure it out and then the tools and strategies in this book will help guide you to make it become reality.

CHAPTER 13

CRITICISM

The more you showcase your talents and passions, the more you will reveal your genuine self. The more you bare your soul, the more the inevitable criticism will come your way...

What am I going to tell you next is important, so highlight it, save it, put it on your bathroom mirror. I need to remind myself of this every day:

Being uncomfortable and sitting in that discomfort is part of being successful.

There was never a successful person that could please everyone and placate all of their critics. To be successful, you will need to learn to accept that there WILL be people out there who won't like you (they may even claim they hate you). There will definitely be people who won't like the way you look, who won't like the things you have to say, and who won't like the work that you create—and will tell you as much. And I am here to let you know: all of that is OKAY. In fact, it is more than okay, because it means you are becoming more you, and you are willing to say what you think in the FACE of potential criticism—as were all great men and women. If you have reached this point in your life, thank you for being genuine and courageous and for allowing yourself to take personal hits in order to change our world.

Increased public criticism can serve as a guidepost to let you know that you are flourishing and growing. As you begin to feel more comfortable with your uniqueness, you will become more polarizing because your work and how you show up in the world will strongly attract some people and opportunities while naturally repelling others.

I am not suggesting that you never listen to criticism, especially the constructive kind with good intentions, nor am I suggesting you be purposefully evocative for the heck of it. I'm saying that you need to learn to sit in the discomfort that comes along with people not liking you and your work. You will never escape criticism if you want to live a life on your terms, so prepare yourself for it.

You will also engender criticism you didn't expect or deserve. This will inevitably happen as you show more of yourself to the world, which is why it's imperative to have an internal sense of value that is completely independent from others' opinions of you.

Criticism is the price you pay for true freedom, so learning how to cope with it is one of the most valuable skills you can cultivate.

A part of my internal sense of value, and the tools I use to manage negative criticism, came from my experience in spending a portion of my life feeling powerless.

As I sit typing this book, my husband is scrolling through Netflix—looking for a good show to binge on a Friday night. I see two shows which instantly trigger some sort of unconscious emotional response; it comes out as a heavy sigh, "Oh".

The two shows are *Laguna Beach* and *The Hills*, there for all of the millions of Netflix users to watch and re-watch. To this day, I have not watched them since they aired, and still cannot bring myself to watch them. It's not like watching them would be that bad, just distinctly unpleasant. I still have no desire to observe myself naively trying to navigate high-school and college life through the lens of other people's dramatic perspectives.

As a minor character on both series from the ages of eighteen to twenty-two, I was the perfect target. My character was pliable enough to mold into whatever was convenient, yet still easy enough to discard when it was time. I wasn't shown on screen enough to make into a likeable "character", but I was aired enough to be made into whatever they wanted me to be. Not popular enough to have a voice or a storyline, but around enough to manipulate into whatever served their purpose at the time. The wing-girl, the boyfriend-stealer, the clueless friend. Whatever worked, right? Not a big deal, right? Until it was.

These shows which aired on national (and international) television were so popular that they actually both became the number one show in the nation for a period of time. At some point, the show's producers decided that they were going to portray me as the up-and-coming designated villain on the second season of *The Hills*. Every story needs a dramatic arc.

As the villain, they made it appear like I had boldly betrayed the beloved protagonist of the show. They needed a token boyfriend stealer, and I was unknowingly chosen to fill those empty shoes. They created this piece of scripted drama in post-production editing, where they patched together scenes from different days and times and incorporated in-studio voice-overs—a common practice in the reality TV world.

During my in-studio voice-overs they wouldn't tell me why they were asking me to say certain things but just what phrases to say into a microphone, which I did. They didn't ask me to say anything outlandish, like "I am stealing your boyfriend," but they used recorded phrases like "goodnight I will see you later" completely out of context to help them make a fake storyline seem real.

These untruths and fake storylines ushering in my new role as "boyfriend stealer" were aired without warning during a new weekly episode, dropping like a bombshell, to millions of viewers. The main characters on the show were able to watch each new episode before it aired each week with a special viewing—as a more minor character, I was not a part of this group. This meant I saw each episode I was featured on, as it aired to millions, like the rest of the world. I remember getting a call from the executive producer of the show, a few minutes before this particular episode aired and he said, "Hey Jen, I just want to call you as a courtesy to let you know you aren't going to like what you see this week." Thanks. There was clearly a lot I could do about it at that point. But he was right, I didn't like it—in fact, I still don't. Unfortunately, all of this occurred before social media and other personal broadcasting channels were popular, so I had few ways to explain to the larger public my side of the story. I had no platform to tell the world that things didn't happen like that, that this didn't represent who I was, or which scenes were totally fabricated. I felt completely blindsided by people who I thought were my friends, both cast and crew.

After the episode attacking my character aired, everything changed. I don't think they, nor I, realized the tremendous reaction and consequences those production decisions would ultimately create. It's both unfair and inaccurate to place blame on anyone for what ended up happening. All of us, together, were naively swept up in the tidal wave of this new form of media—fake reality—and with it came the uncertainty of knowing just how drastically it would change our lives.

A few months after that episode aired, a couple of friends and I ventured to Cabo San Lucas, Mexico, for our spring break. What could go wrong, right? We were celebrating life, as college students do, dancing and having a great time at a popular night club, when I suddenly heard a glass bottle shatter right next to me. Sharp shards of glass glittered on the ground all around me just centimeters from my open-toed sandals and bare legs. Then I heard obscenities called out in my direction. I didn't put two and two together until a few minutes later when another bottle hit me (thankfully plastic this time), followed by more obscenities. It turned out that perfect strangers recognized me from the show and decided that I deserved to be harassed on my spring break. That's when I realized how serious the situation really was; fake media had physical ramifications. I couldn't ignore it anymore. The effects from this fake reality TV episode were translating into real emotional harm and physical danger, and on an international scale.

At first, I had perceived myself as somewhat insulated from it all, with the show functioning as nothing more than an interesting but minor side hobby during my quest to finish college at USC. However, I quickly realized that the situation was bigger—much bigger than I could have ever anticipated. I was completely out of my league. The show blew up, as did my notorious reputation and I didn't have the tools I needed as a young adult to cope with it all. I was ill-equipped to handle the backlash and vitriol—including death threats from internet strangers and hurtful comments from people in my own community—that came with an unfair character assassination playing out on a national stage.

I even had a college professor pulling me aside and commenting about the untruths aired on the show. The very last corner of the earth I thought this would reach, my pre-med classroom, was now sullied by this mess. I was harassed by strangers, and even acquaintances, on the internet and in real life. Suffice it to say that "boyfriend stealer" was one of the nicer names I was called.

My parents were never supportive of my participation in reality television in the first place. I rebelled and went against their wishes to even sign the contract. They were worried it would interfere with my career ambitions to become a doctor, so when I had this huge negative event happen, I tried to hide it. I felt embarrassed to go to them for support.

While I know I'm not the only one who has gone through difficult situations as a young adult, for me, at that age, the whole experience was a shock to my system. It felt like others were judging a character on television instead of the real person in front of them. I felt like I had no voice and no one to go to for advice on how to handle it. I really believed that I had no power. It was a form of modern gaslighting. I was stuck, without recourse, and without a way to counter their manufactured version of reality. There was no way I could yell, "That's not true"—other than at my dog, Rainbow, who would often look up at me with sympathy. At times, it felt like the world was against me. You might even say the world WAS against me.

So, how does feeling powerless and receiving death threats give you confidence and lead to success?

A few years later in my mid-twenties, when the dust had finally settled, I was able to recognize that this experience transformed me. The whole ordeal brought me to a low point, but simultaneously it made me impervious to negativity from others. This has benefitted me to this day and it has served as one of my most profound learning experiences. Forced to cope with the fallout of the situation alone, I realized how strong I was. Having public opinion turned against me with only the support of myself and close friends, I learned that this type of support was the only support that ever mattered.

Other people's opinions of my characters didn't change my character—it only made me stronger.

Going through this experience during a formative period in my life certainly wasn't a walk in the park, but now, as an adult, I am a force to reckon with! I have learned how to strongly advocate for myself and not be taken advantage of. Most importantly, I gained the confidence to understand that my real value didn't come from "out there." It didn't come from strangers, and it certainly didn't come from the internet. It came from me.

I am no longer scared to put myself out there. I am not scared of people judging, criticizing, or commenting negatively on my work. I am not scared of trying and losing. I am not addicted to being liked by strangers (it is usually fleeting), nor am I opposed to being disliked by strangers (it's usually fleeting as well). I know I can cope with almost anything that comes my way. I can handle a tremendous amount of rejection and negativity, and because of that I am willing to take risks in areas that are important to me. I know through experience (and this is now what I teach my kids to practice daily) that I CAN do hard things. And I promise, so can you.

A thick skin together with true, internal confidence is not something that can be taught, it needs to be experienced. And while you don't have to get bashed on reality television to get there, I recommend that you put yourself out there as often as you possibly can so that you can fail, fail, and fail again. Yes, FAIL! It changes you. When you fail, you usually have someone tell you, for lack of better words, that you suck, and you can choose to believe it or persevere and let the experience ignite your drive and internal confidence.

The failures, hardships, and bad days will be your greatest lessons—the lessons that teach you to love yourself for who you are and value yourself for the things YOU know to be true. The skills you learn in times of failure and rejection will be your guiding light throughout your life.

CHAPTER 14

IMPERFECTION

We are defined by our challenges and our shortcomings. I love the saying, "Your mess is your message," but we don't need to experience life-changing tragedy or trauma to have a message. Who we are is what we've learned from what has happened to us. Our experiences dictate how we decide to bring those lessons into the future to change our behavior and, hopefully, the actions of others for the better.

There were times in my life where I felt invincible; everything was going right, and the more things that were going right, the stronger and more unshakeable I was. Then, there were the times I felt weak, vulnerable, and so fragile that any minor upset could send me into a tailspin. I felt like a leaf in the proverbial wind. Mostly, the weak times centered around the birth of my children and the major emotional, physical, and lifestyle changes that come with a new family member. Although I felt weak during these moments—these were also the times where I drew from my most enduring strength and realized my most valuable lessons.

Sitting in discomfort is the process of allowing something that's uncomfortable to happen because it needs to process. We can sit in discomfort with emotions, with physical pain, and even with grief.

Stop for a second and really think about the two to three things in your life that have brought you to your knees, to the darkest places, and were the hardest to overcome. Those are probably also the two to three things that shaped you into becoming more resilient, empathetic, stronger, and better able to help others at a level that you couldn't have reached otherwise. Never regret or be ashamed of those experiences, and don't be afraid to use those experiences to drive you, connect with others, and use the lessons to define how you want to show up in the world.

I always thought that when I "grew up" and became an adult I would live that perfect life I had always envisioned. The one with the perfect routine, the perfectly groomed and well-behaved kids, and the nice house. But becoming a mom quickly taught me that the pristine, neat, clean, and perfectly run household I had envisioned just wasn't going to happen.

I had envisioned purchasing my home and the birth of my first child as the real beginning to adult life where all of the ideas I had in my head of obtaining perfection would come true. When I moved into my first home at five months pregnant, we decorated and got ready for the baby by preparing the most beautiful nursery. I also started working from home at my dream job. I have to admit, I felt like things were pretty under control. It almost seemed as if my vision for my adult life was conforming itself to reality. But I was wrong. Soon, all hell broke loose.

It started with labor. The baby didn't come on time, and I was forced to be induced at almost forty-two weeks. The labor started off innocently enough—they gave me an induction pill to kick off my contractions, and kick them off it did. I started contracting so hard and fast that my baby's heart rate was decelerating. It became an instant emergency and was one of the most terrifying moments of my life. I was given a strong medicine in the form of a shot to reverse the overzealous contractions. The medicine made me sick, but thankfully my baby was okay. I was grateful. I then labored for almost forty hours.

At the end of my labor, I started bleeding profusely and needed another strong (and, I later learned, somewhat dangerous) medication to stop the bleeding. Unfortunately, I ended up having a serious reaction to the medication and my heart was affected. I remember being unable to stand long enough to take a shower at the hospital without my heart beating at what felt like a hundred miles a minute. But since it was my first baby, I assumed I was just fatigued and it was normal. I was cleared for discharge from the hospital a few days later. I was so focused on the baby and so blissfully happy to go home after everything that had happened, I really wasn't thinking about myself physically. Even though I was discharged from the hospital, I knew in my gut that something was off.

I was having chest pains, trouble breathing, walking, and getting around the house. A day later, I began to feel worse. I was sitting on the couch with my four-day-old baby when, all of a sudden, my heart started going unexplainably fast, as if I was running a marathon uphill. My body felt like it was paralyzed and turning into ice. My vision started collapsing into black. Instantly, I knew something was wrong. It was a feeling I had never experienced before in my life, but it was one of those moments where you know, without a doubt, you are in the middle of an emergency.

Luckily, I had my mom there and I told her to call 911. I had never called 911 before, but I didn't hesitate for a second. Something was going horribly wrong inside of me and I knew it. I ended up in the ER, and we found out that I had a pericardial effusion (water around my heart) likely caused by the combination of long labor and the medications. Fortunately, I was not admitted into the hospital at that time and was able to rest and heal at home. It was later found that I also had the beginning stages of postpartum HELLP syndrome, a dangerous form of preeclampsia.

Because of these complications, I didn't get to have the labor I had envisioned, nor did I get to spend those first few months with my baby in the way that I had imagined I would my whole life. Almost immediately, my vision for the type of mom (and person) I wanted to be was destroyed. It was destroyed because I was too sick to hold my baby, and I was too traumatized from the whole experience to even want to be a mom. All those ideas of a perfect adult existence were gone; this real version was messy, painful and terrifying.

I remember waking up one morning alone, after my husband had already gone to work, and hearing my son cry. I went into his nursery and picked him up from the crib to change his diaper—something simple that every decent mom should be able to do, right? But as I stood there changing his diaper, it started—racing heart, trouble breathing, starting to feel faint. I had to put him back in his crib quickly, without a diaper, before I fainted. I laid on the floor of his nursery until my heart calmed down enough to stand up again. I felt like I had failed as a mom; I couldn't even change my newborn's diaper, something everyone expected me to do seamlessly.

I was frustrated, overwhelmed, scared, and broken. This was supposed to be a sacred time with my first-born child. This was supposed to be my chance to be the mom I had always dreamt I would be—and I couldn't even stand up. My inability to function as a mom during this time due to my health issues was both physically immobilizing and mentally incapacitating.

I am very fortunate that my health issues eventually resolved later that year, as I know some moms aren't so lucky, but the impact of that experience on me is permanent.

I was faced with this fact of life: bad things can happen to you, and they can happen quickly and without warning. My version of reality (and my vision for motherhood) didn't initially allow for that. I was shown, like a slap in the face, how imperfect life could be and there was nothing that I could do about it—or even know it was coming. This was my first serious reality check and it showed me that life isn't necessarily going to go my way, even when it comes to the big things.

Looking back, I wish I had reacted differently to those events in the early days of motherhood. I wish I dealt with the situation with more grace and resilience. I wish I had been more optimistic and positive instead of breaking down and losing it. I wish I had been stronger for my son and my family and not fallen apart through all of the medical emergencies I endured. After that experience, I recognized the truth—the perfect life doesn't exist. But in that experience, I also realized that I can do my best through trauma, through tragedy, through frightening and difficult times to allow for a real version of perfection to evolve. For me, real perfection means doing my personal best and sometimes allowing myself the space to figuratively wilt, die, and then rebirth in order to evolve.

I was not able to show up for my son the way I wanted to in the first year after his birth. My perfect home has now been taken over by toddlers. My white couches and chairs have been destroyed, in addition to several other (read: all other) expensive items. I have not accomplished many of the things I thought I would have by this season in life. I say all of this to illustrate that, despite our very best efforts and intentions, we need to leave room for life to happen. Because it will. The great, the miraculous, the tragic, the terrifying, the messy, and the unexpected.

Work with imperfection, not against it.

When we try a new routine, start a new job, or enter into a new stage of life, we want things to go according to plan. We envision a consistent commitment to an exercise program, or meditating for fifteen minutes a day without any disruptions, or becoming the perfect mom, partner, employee, business owner, etc. But, as we soon find out, life usually won't bend to the vision in our heads.

It seems, sometimes (if not often), that something always gets in the way of accomplishing a task according to plan. That's not bad luck or a bad day, that's just life. There are screaming kids, rainy days, fatigue, accidents, and countless other "surprises."

Understanding the reality of imperfection will help us set expectations and allow for flexibility. For example, if you wanted to work out five days a week for an hour and you are only getting in twenty-five minutes a day, consider that a win. If you are trying to eat healthier but can only manage to get in a few extra veggies a day, that is also a win.

Perfection is the enemy of complete. If we strive to achieve perfection, we will never reach it. So, instead, I aim to reach sloppy, loose perfection—perfection in the real world. For me, this real-life perfection looks like adjusting at least one to two things every day to meet my personal needs or meet the reality of the environment (for instance, when my kid wants to play with me during the only thirty-minute interval I have all day to work out).

The end goal is to approach or approximate the vision of your day (or life) in your head, not to reach that vision perfectly. Because perfection, quite simply, doesn't exist. Perfection is never tangible. It is a moving goal post that never stops moving further and further away the closer you get to it. That is why becoming a perfectionist is endlessly frustrating. The sooner you can realize what perfection means in reality, the easier it will be to recognize and enjoy the success you have and the success you will achieve in the future.

CHAPTER 15

GRATITUDE AND ATTITUDE

I would like to think I am extremely objective when it comes to who I associate with in my work and personal life. But the truth is, I'm not, and I don't think most people are. Many of the decisions regarding who I decide to engage with simply come down to whether or not I like the person.

With all of the stressors in life, I appreciate people who enjoy life and bring that joy into our relationship, whether personal or professional. Coming across and interacting with a genuinely happy and positive person can easily become the best part of my week. I bask in other people's positive energy, and when I am around people with these qualities, I tend to be healthier and more creative, relaxed, and peaceful.

Amazingly, even with those incredible benefits that we get from happy, positive people, we often aren't intentional about surrounding ourselves with those people, nor are we always intentional about becoming one of those people. You might ask what this has to do with being successful and creating the life of your dreams; this piece is not only important but critical to moving your vision forward.

First, I am not suggesting to be overly bubbly (read: annoying) or disingenuous, but simply to show you are happy to be somewhere and excited to engage with whatever is going on. I cannot tell you how many times I have decided to work with someone with a weaker skill set or less experience because my interactions with them felt positive, and I cannot understate the impact your attitude has on your ability to be successful.

An attitude is like a magnet; it can either attract or repel. You want it to attract, in a genuine way. If you find that you are not a naturally positive person, try out these strategies and see if you can allow this trial to become a habit and then become a part of your character. For some people, this simple shift is life changing.

The best way to shift, if only for a short period of time, into a lighter, more upbeat mindset is to practice gratitude (stay with me here). I have heard about the practice of gratitude for a long, long time, and to be honest, whenever I hear someone telling me to practice gratitude or to name three things for which I am grateful in a gratitude journal, I cringe. I think, not this again, please.

But then, I have these moments, and they are these pivotal moments where something big and usually awful happens in our world: A friend loses a parent or endures the incomprehensible loss of a baby, a natural disaster kills thousands, there is a fatal shooting at a preschool. In these moments, I am flooded with the uncontrolled, overwhelming, raw emotion of GENUINE gratitude—and it changes me, it changes everything. This is where we start.

So, I am not asking you to write down three things in a journal every day, like "I am grateful for my coffee." While it is certainly wonderful to be grateful for your coffee, that simply isn't the type of gratitude that changes your soul. What I am referring to is the type of gratitude that allows you to feel deep empathy for the human condition, while simultaneously being aware of your blessed state. This type of gratitude is unmistakable—when you are feeling it, you know. It feels like a tidal wave of thankfulness and appreciation so strong it's hard to define.

It can be emotionally draining to experience this level of gratitude, while also feeling the sting of empathy, so I don't recommend practicing this every day. But the DEPTH of this gratitude is what will change you. So, while it may be emotionally draining and overwhelming, that's exactly what's shifting your perspective as a human being. The result is a change in how you engage with everything in your world. You'll emanate more positivity, more acceptance, tolerance, love, and success—and other people will not only notice it, they will feel it. If you are able to, practicing this type of gratitude just once a week can permanently shift you into this new state.

This type of gratitude is such a deep awareness of your fortunate state in the world that it drives almost every interaction you have. You won't only change yourself when you operate from this depth, you will change many of the people you interact with.

Sometimes, all it takes is ONE pivotal experience to tap into this level of gratefulness. My dear friend told me she took a trip to South America for a month where she witnessed abject poverty in a small rural village. Children didn't have food or medicine. They slept on dirty floors. Some lost their lives. For her, that experience became the moment that she shifted into permanent gratitude.

Another friend of mine ventured into the depths of the Amazon to live with the indigenous tribes. He, too, was fundamentally changed through the gratitude that experience evoked, but even more amazing, he was changed by the gratitude the tribe had for their lives. They were as happy as could be, even without basic access to food, healthcare or running water.

Obviously, we all can't pick up and travel to have these life-changing experiences, but if you are having trouble connecting with positivity and joy in your life and relationships, then try to immerse yourself in this raw gratitude. Local volunteering, education through reading about what others have endured, and philanthropic travel are all ways to have these meaningful experiences.

At one point, most of us have had the experience of extreme gratitude, whether it came from a movie, a book, a death, a loss, or even a story in the news. The goal is to be able to make this perspective shift a permanent part of your life. Once this shift occurs, it will be difficult not to show up for people in your life with a big, genuine, toothy smile. You will find yourself having a harder time finding things to complain about. You might also find yourself more interested in others, and less interested in your own personal situation. You will begin attracting people who value positivity into your life, which will ultimately set you up to be far more successful and closer to your ideal life vision than you would have ever been otherwise.

Extreme gratitude is a lifestyle change. The effects of extreme gratitude can often be felt through generations, and across communities. Be the starting point. Be the extreme gratitude domino that affects every other piece in its path. The rewards resulting from this type of shift in your life are frankly, endless.

CHAPTER 16

TRUST

A part of achieving big goals is being able to trust those around us to do some of the work. It could be anyone from a coworker, to a friend, to a partner. We have to be able to delegate some of our responsibilities to other people in order to focus on our priorities.

At one point, I was micromanaging my nanny, my coworkers, my husband, and even the neighborhood kid who walks our dog. I had to remember that even if someone else didn't do the task perfectly, delegating that task was better than having it steal my attention and focus away from my true priorities.

Total, hands-off delegation in some areas of your life for certain periods of time is a prerequisite to success. Of course, just like everything else, that's easier said than done, which is why we need to practice loosening up the reins and giving up control in some areas so that we can fully devote ourselves to others.

For type A personalities and over-achievers, delegating is going to be hard. This is why those who seek control often have a hard time with meditation because in essence they are giving up control of their mind for a short period of time. However, I have learned this imperative: **the ability to let go is as important as the drive to succeed.**

A strategy to help you practice this life skill is first allowing for less control in areas that you don't care about as much. For me, this meant letting my husband do the nightly dishes on his terms. This often meant waiting until the next day to put away the dishes that were "drying" (read: could have dried off with a dish towel but didn't want to). Despite the flaws, this allowed me at least thirty extra minutes a night to spend time with the kids, finish up extra work, or simply put my feet up.

After successfully delegating this task completely, I started to realize the benefits of fully passing off work, without worrying whether or not it would get done or get done in the way I had envisioned. From there, I delegated larger tasks until I only had a core set of tasks that I either wanted to do myself (like take my kids to swimming lessons) or had to do myself (like write this book).

You may be surprised by how many tasks you can outsource, allowing you to spend that time on high-value activities. If outsourcing feels frivolous or luxurious at first, that is totally normal, but give it a try. Sometimes, it actually helps you focus—kind of like when you pay for an exercise class you are more likely to show up.

For many years, I refused to have someone else clean my home. I thought, what a waste of money; I can do that! But then I realized that not only can a professional do it better and in half of the time, but I am also providing them with income while I get to spend my time doing something that will continue to provide me with dividends for a long time to come.

When you start delegating, your remaining core set of tasks should only be things that are either important to you personally or that only you can do. This allows you to maximize your time in a way that makes you simultaneously feel more productive and more fulfilled. It might seem hard at first, but delegating is something you can learn to have fun with, and once you fall into a pattern of fully trusting other people to do the things you don't want to do, it will be hard to ever go back. Happy delegating!

CHAPTER 17

THE SUCCESS SCARIES

I see so many people who are afraid to reach their potential because they are afraid of what their success will bring with it and what it will mean. I have seen "success fright" as one of the major reasons for brilliant, passionate people continuing to play small. I do not define the word success throughout this book because it means drastically different things to different people. Traditionally, people equate success with financial gains or material assets, but success is not necessarily a number or an object; there are innumerable definitions of success, and they are not mutually exclusive. Success can mean recognition, fame, happiness, health, financial freedom, a good marriage, making an impact in whatever it is you do (including the very valuable and important task of raising children!), and more.

Some people feel that if they are successful that means other people cannot be. But success is not a zero-sum game. We need to think of achieving success as equivalent to **creating value**, and more for all, not less.

We may also make the mistake of associating financial success with greed, pushing us further away from making money. While in some cases that may be true, in most cases making money is about **value creation**. For example, if you start a small business and it grows, it's likely because you are creating value for your customers. Your customers are willing to pay you money in order to receive your goods or services because it will leave them better off than without them. In exchange, you receive money from your customer, which you can then use to buy consumer goods (improving the economy by giving other people money in exchange for something valuable or essential to you), investing (earning equity and/or helping yours or other businesses grow), or saving. Your income, profits, or sales are taxed, which means that a portion of what you make will go to creating better roads and infrastructure, ultimately benefiting everyone. Of course, this is a simplified example, but you can see how your profits and financial success isn't taking success away from others. Instead, your success is continuing to create more value.

Don't apologize for your success. As counterintuitive as it may seem, many people are ashamed of their success. Sometimes people feel that they don't deserve it, or that they don't want to appear to have more than others. Some people feel bad if they have achieved things that others have not. This is especially likely if your parents struggled and you grew up with humble beginnings. For some, suffering and working hard to make ends meet is considered a badge of honor. If you grew up in this type of environment and then you begin to reach a place where you feel comfortable with finances, you may even feel like you've done something wrong.

Feeling ashamed of your success will not help you gain more of it. Even more harmful, shame limits you from achieving your true potential. While you should continue to be of service and attuned to others' circumstances in life, you do not have to apologize for your success, and you do not have to feel guilty for being given opportunities in any form, including luck, money, education, or access to certain people. In this next exercise, we will explore negative beliefs about success, and how we can work with them so we can reach our true potential without fear.

Exercise 8: Rebooting Success

You might be scared of success for many reasons such as anxiety about the changes success will bring in your life, fear of failing and losing it all, social anxiety about what others might think, or even guilt about the very idea of success.

If any of these reasons resonate with you, try to zero in on what exactly is driving your fear so that we can dive into questioning those assumptions.

Answer the below questions with complete honesty.

- Are there certain people that you think might judge you or feel badly if you gain success?
- Who are they?
- Are their judgments or bad feelings real or are you guessing that is how they *might* feel?
- What is your relationship like with them?
- On average, is your relationship with them healthy or toxic?
- Do you feel unworthy of success?
- If so, when did you start to feel that way?
- Can you remember the first time you ever felt unworthy of success?
- What were the circumstances in your life at the time when you felt unworthy of success?

The more deeply you can explore where your fears of success originate from, the easier they will become to untangle and tame. Awareness of your fears will also make it easier to recognize when they show up in your life so that you can stop perpetuating them. For some, recognition of these fears is enough to eliminate them altogether. Others will need to engage in some further work to address these issues, especially if these fears are deeply rooted.

Gaining Success and Reaching your Peak

Sometimes, when you reach success (however you define it), you will feel like you have FINALLY achieved what you set out to do! This realization is usually followed by elation, happiness, relief, and then . . . anxiety, boredom, discomfort, and unhappiness.

You then may find yourself in the uncomfortable spot of having to define a whole new set of post-success goals, not knowing what is or what should be next for you. I know a person whose only goal was to get married, be a mom, and have a family. But, once her kids went to school and needed her less, she found herself needing to redefine what she wanted next in life. This can happen with CEOs who reach the pinnacle of their career, and even with presidents of the United States who have to figure out what they want from life once their presidential term is over.

The more focused you have been, and the harder you have worked to get where you are, the more challenging it may be to set new goals once you've reached the proverbial "top of the mountain." This mountaintop is where I see a lot of successful, brilliant, talented people stagnate. They think, well I have worked my whole life to get here, and now I am here. What now? I can't just take vacation for the next ten or twenty years.

On one hand, you might feel like you have finally accomplished enough, so you want to slow down and relax. But on the other hand, you feel restless and experience the need to accomplish even more (will it ever stop?).

This pinnacle moment is an opportunity to look within and re-examine the core values that have led you to your first set of goals. Have those core values shifted? Sometimes we find that we focused our first set of goals on mostly material wealth or status, such as achieving a certain income level, size of house, professional title, brand of car, or societal status in life. When we reach those goals, we might experience an appetite to achieve different goals—acts of service, spiritual connection, spending more time with family, or working on creative endeavors. These goals are not necessarily mutually exclusive with material achievements, and it is okay if they overlap!

Some people find it difficult to re-examine their goals because they have so long prioritized their first set of goals for such a large portion of their life that it is challenging to shift their focus. For some, this shift feels like admitting to themselves that they were wrong all along. But I see this shift differently; I see it as growth and evolution, not as having taken a wrong first direction. I see it as getting closer to self-actualization, and to your highest potential as a human being. Re-examining your goals and values, even after tremendous success, is an admirable step in self-evolution. May we all be courageous enough to embark on that journey when the time is right.

CHAPTER 18

TIME

The most common rationalizations people make when attempting to implement the suggestions in this book is a perceived lack of time. I am here to tell you that you can actually "bend" time to make it work for you. Sound crazy? Hold your disbelief and let me explain.

Why is it that, for most people, time seems to go slowly when you are a child, and then when you're an adult, time suddenly starts flying by. For me, five years as an adult feels like a few months as a child. The years seem to be racking up so fast it's hard to know how to slow them down.

I have spoken to countless parents who feel like they blinked and their children were fully grown. Yet, when we are younger, we can distinctly remember each grade at school, our teachers, the details of how we felt in certain conversations, or what we wore.

I believe part of the answer to this time discrepancy has to do with the amount of creative space we allow for ourselves as children versus as adults. Play time, art, music, as well as socializing, all expand time. This time for creative space allows us to pay attention to our surroundings, to concentrate on the details, to notice the little things. Have you heard the saying, "See the world through a child's eyes"? Part of expanding time is doing this as an adult. Paradoxically, if you want to create "more" time, it requires taking more time for yourself, to play, and to make room for creative expression. Once you begin to do this, you will likely notice your perception of time expanding.

Another way to create more time is to look at how you are currently spending it. List out how you are spending each hour of your day or each day of the week. You might be surprised how much of your time is spent mindlessly scrolling or watching television.

Taking a screen diet can give you back so much of your life; it is hard to recognize just how much until you try it. One of my guidelines is to limit screens when I am in the middle of big projects I want to complete. The screen rest also helps me break any habitual practices of flipping on the TV or looking at my Instagram when I feel tired. Instead, my screen rule encourages me to continue engaging my brain in healthy but lower energy activities, like reading.

Another strategy for creating more time is to transition where you are working. How would changing where you work create more time? If you make a ritual out of working in a designated place outside of your normal workspace for important projects, you can actually focus for longer and complete things more quickly, creating more time. It also can spark creativity!

An example of this practice in action is going to get your favorite latte, then setting up at the coffee shop where you can look forward to a delicious pastry while you work. This strategy not only gives you motivation, it also helps establish a habit of positively associating that location with focus and productivity. It is important not to do much else in that location but work on a specific, high-value project (and eat/drink) because the goal is to strengthen the association between focus and your new location. This is also why sleep researchers suggest that the bedroom is only for sex and sleep; it's the same concept. Your brain makes strong associations with completing certain activities in specific places. If you can make positive associations with the place, you will be more inclined to show up. We can take this phenomenon and use it to our advantage to achieve more productivity and save time.

Once you establish a strong association with your new designated work spot, you will notice that when you go to that place, you are more likely to engage productively in that high-value activity. If you try this, it only takes a few days to notice a change and create a more focused, location-based habit. I particularly recommend this strategy for projects that require a lot of sustained focused, and creativity (like writing), but it works for almost anything.

I installed a swinging egg chair on my front porch and it is probably the most lucrative purchase I have ever made. I designated that swing my "working place" and when I go out and sit in that chair my head clears and I can immediately focus for ten times longer than I can in my office. I find myself more creative and better at problem-solving when I am sitting in my swing. When I get into that swing, I often find myself lost in the work instead of looking at my phone. Find *your* special place. It may take a little bit of trial and error but you'll soon make a lot of headway; be sure to complete only your high-value work projects in whichever place you end up designating as your special work space.

I would love to hear how this goes for you! You will notice that by becoming focused you actually "create" more time in your day because you are able to complete your high-value projects (which you have prioritized on your to-do list) in only a fraction of the time.

Tips for finding a great designated work place:

- Choose a space that makes you feel relaxed.
- Ensure you do not pick somewhere busy—you don't want constant distractions.
- Select a spot with a lot of natural light (artificial light, or a darker environment can make you feel lethargic).

- Choose a place filled with nature. Being surrounded by nature has been proven to be associated with improved cognitive functioning, increased attention, creativity and better mood.

- Pick somewhere where you can get comfortable. Working for long hours requires a comfortable place to sit, or perhaps to put up your feet.

CHAPTER 19

LAST CALL:
TIPS AND HABITS

There are a few habits that have helped me tremendously. I picked these up from experts, books, family, friends, and experience. These habits have helped make my life both easier and more productive. They have brought me more joy, greater satisfaction, and an overall sense of well-being. I hope that they can provide the same for you.

Physical Health: The Body

No matter what, prioritize your health. This means fresh, organic food, daily exercise, sunlight/air, and sleep. These are not nice-to-haves; this is the raw fuel driving your performance, your value, your success, and, most importantly, your personal happiness.

There is rarely anything I'll let get in the way of meeting my health priorities. This is because I value myself, and I know that without these essential building blocks I will not be my best self and therefore, cannot offer my best to others. These elements will make you ten times more productive; taking care of your physical and mental health is the exact same thing as prioritizing your success in life.

- **Working out**

Try and exercise no matter what—as long as you are feeling well. Exercise can look different for everyone, but the main ingredient is moving your body. You don't have to work out in the traditional way, you can exercise in any way that works for you. This could mean taking a walk, playing tennis, doing some yoga, attending a dance class, or going hiking. Studies show that people who don't move around a lot because they have a sedentary day job or just enjoy their couch end up with double the mortality risk when all other factors have been controlled for. So, continue to move your body no matter what else is going on.

Exercise before cleaning the floor, exercise before folding the laundry, exercise before anything that isn't an emergency because, while your house may be dirtier, your body is going to be healthier for it. Your health is not something you can outsource or make someone else's responsibility and it will impact you (and your family) for the rest of your life. So, try and make exercise a constant, and dedicated priority.

If you have a job that requires you to sit in front of a computer, you can introduce walking meetings (my favorite type of meeting). On numerous occasions, I have told people that I cannot make a video call but will be able to participate on the phone. The reason? I wanted to make it a walking meeting. Now, this isn't always possible with every obligation you have, but try to walk around and move as much as you possibly can (walking your dog, catching up with friends, playing with your kids, meetings, walking while listening to an audiobook, etc.). Studies clearly show a reduced disease burden and improved all-around health for people who are able to walk in excess of ten thousand steps per day. This might seem like a difficult number to reach on a daily basis, but with a little creativity, you'll discover it's possible.

Of course, I am not always successful, but here is my general strategy for reaching those five-digit step counts. I walk uphill or run for thirty minutes in the morning to give my steps a jumpstart for the day. This ends up motivating me for the remainder of the day because I get off to such a good start. Then, I take up to three walking meetings a day, killing two birds with one stone. I also try to walk the dog on a long walk each day, and I will often try to take an additional walk in the evening with my husband and kids. This allows me (without any other additional exercise) to get close to that ten thousand step mark.

I know price and space are limiting factors, but if you have the resources to invest in a basic treadmill, I highly recommend it. I use mine several times per day in the summer months when it is too hot to comfortably walk outside. Owning a treadmill allows your step count to remain consistent when weather offers obstacles. You can also complete other sedentary activities (working/reading) on a treadmill. My treadmill is probably one of the most utilized purchases in my entire household. Just a note, if you have kids, make sure you follow treadmill safety guidelines to keep everyone in your house safe.

Additionally, I try not to sit for more than ninety minutes at a time. Sitting for many consecutive hours of work is associated with a variety of health issues, including stroke, dementia, and heart disease. For links to these studies and more visit my website www.drjendunphy.com, or follow me on social media @drjendunphy.

- **Brrrrrr**

This next tip is not unique and many have suggested it, but it really works so I wanted to include it here. I take at least a thirty second cold shower in the morning. It gets my brain working and my body buzzing and refreshes me in a way nothing else does. Those thirty seconds prepare me for the day. The best result occurs if I can last a minute or more in the cold water. If I have to wash my hair, I will often make the first thirty seconds a cold shower before switching to a regular warm/hot shower for the remaining time. However, I have found transitioning to warm water only gives me a fraction of the benefits that cold showers only do. So, if you want the biggest impact, try cold only first. Some people can last for a very long time in the cold water, which is impressive! I am not yet one of those people…

- **Spinach for breakfast?**

This tip is going to sound odd, but I love starting off my day eating spinach. It makes me feel great. Spinach has vitamins like A, C, K, potassium, iron, and folate that help fuel my body all day long. I try to incorporate one handful of spinach into my food by noon. I will do this by making a one egg omelet with spinach and a dash of cheese, or by throwing a handful of spinach into my smoothie (I usually pre-make my smoothies and store them in the freezer). You can find my recipes online on Instagram @drjendunphy and on my website www.drjendunphy.com.

- **Vitamin D**

Getting Vitamin D before 10 a.m., both orally and through sunlight, can provide major health benefits. I will take vitamin D pills and then follow that up with a walk outside (weather permitting). Taking a walk in the morning and having the sunlight hit your pupils helps organize your circadian clock (helping you sleep better). Evidence also shows that Vitamin D helps prevent many chronic diseases, including cancers, cardiac disease, and neurological problems. For more information on these studies, visit me on my Instagram @drjendunphy or my website www.drjendunphy.com.

- **Rest & Relax**

When I am tired, I rest. This means making time to sleep if there is a need and making sure all variables are in place to ensure a good rest (for me, these variables are a sound machine, a cooling mattress pad, and a pitch-black room). It is not always easy, but it's vital to attune to our body's rhythms. Remember, your body gets fatigued when it is fighting infections or trying to repair itself (and in children when they are growing). Research has even shown that you repair DNA damage while you sleep. So, whenever I feel tired, I remind myself that my body needs rest to stay healthy.

We have a culture of getting up earlier and earlier in an attempt to do more. Sleeping few hours has become a badge of honor. This labels sleep as the enemy, but that couldn't be further from the truth. Needing rest does NOT mean you are lazy or unmotivated or unsuccessful. In fact, the opposite is true. Sleep is vital, sleep is your life source, sleep is what keeps you on your game. We literally cannot survive without sleep. The more you listen to your body, the more your body will listen to you when you want energy, good sleep, and focus. You are your body, and your body is you—it's a bidirectional relationship. Get the rest you need and do not feel guilty about it. While others may not understand why you need a nap or why you need to go to bed early, you know that you are taking care of your body so that you can be the healthiest, happiest version of yourself. Because of the critical role sleep has when it comes to health, I set firm and unassailable boundaries around protecting rest, such as: not waking anyone up unless it is an emergency, consistent bed times, and quiet time during sleep hours. With two toddlers this isn't easy, but with practice and modeling reverence around sleep, we have found it possible.

For access to studies on the importance of sleep—including its ability to fight cancer and obesity and chronic disease, go to my website www.drjendunphy.com or follow me on social media @drjendunphy.

- **Internal Morning Bath**

I take what I call an "inside bath" in the mornings. This means drinking one and a half full glasses of water immediately upon waking up. After brushing my teeth, that's the first thing that I do, no matter what. After a night without water, your body is dehydrated. Drinking will help hydrate your cells and give you energy for whatever comes next—even if that's consuming dehydrating caffeine!

- **Variety in Food**

My overall goal in my diet is not to consume too much of any one thing. I attempt to make my diet as varied as possible, so I try not to eat the same type of food several days in a row (with the exception of my coffee!). I don't restrict anything specifically, other than processed foods and food that is high in sugar (most of the time). I eat homemade pasta, homemade pizza, cheese, and sometimes, homemade cookies! I eat what makes me feel good and gives me energy.

I believe that your body can tell you what it needs, so if you feel like you need salt, eat salt, and when you feel like you need sugar, eat that, too. There is even evidence that when you engage in cognitively complex tasks that your body craves more sugar. Why? Because your brain needs sugar (glucose) AND fats to function well! So, for all those people constantly restricting themselves, try giving into your cravings (with healthy, whole foods), in moderation, and see if you feel different. Your body just might be telling you what it needs to operate most efficiently. My only rule is to stick to clean, fresh foods (this means organic and non-processed for the most part).

If you would like to learn more about what foods are healthiest and which contain toxins, feel free to check out *The Toxin Handbook*, available on my website, www.drjendunphy.com/books.

- **Fasting**

I am a fan of intermittent fasting, although I did it long before it became a trend. My intermittent fasting habit came about via a trial-and-error period spent figuring out what makes me feel my best. The reason I practice intermittent fasting is not to lose weight, it's because I notice that when I eat breakfast (even healthy breakfast), I start to lose energy and focus. So, I usually fast in the morning, with the exception of my coffee, until I complete my workout and any tasks that require a lot of brain power. It sounds counterintuitive to not eat in the mornings (breakfast is the most important meal of the day, right?), but it works really for some people.

I will usually eat breakfast around eleven, or sometimes I will skip breakfast altogether and wait until lunch. When I have my smoothies, I also wait until about ten-thirty or eleven to drink them. I like to keep things very minimal in the early morning because that is what makes me feel my personal best.

There is no guarantee you will feel good doing the same things as I do, but I do recommend you experiment with when eating makes you feel good and when it makes you feel sluggish and tired. I am suggesting this with the underlying assumption that what you are eating is going to be mainly vegetable-based, non-processed food. Otherwise, WHAT you are eating and not WHEN you are eating is going to be a huge confounding factor in figuring out what fasting period (if any) works for you. Always check with a medical doctor first before trying any new diet.

Personally, fasting fills me with energy and I look forward to that clean feeling where my body can rest from digesting, but fasting doesn't work for everyone, so always do what feels right for you.

Mental Health: The Mind

- **Enjoy!**

Do something you look forward to every single day. When you are done with the minimum schedule, celebrate the accomplishment! I am admittedly and unabashedly indulgent with my "treats."

Treats can be anything from watching your favorite show, getting a massage, going out to lunch with a friend, or doing yoga in your backyard. Don't let a day go by without treating yourself to something YOU genuinely love doing. This doesn't have to be something expensive—it can be something as simple as letting yourself relax and laugh for an hour.

- **Chaotic Space, Chaotic Mind**

Keep things organized. Nothing makes me feel more in control of my environment like organizing. I didn't used to be an organized person. In fact, I used to be rather disorganized when I was younger. Then, all of a sudden, I became addicted. Now everything has a spot and a label. If you haven't tried living an organized lifestyle, you are in for a treat.

Organization reduces external chaos which, in turn, reduces internal chaos, and don't we all want that? I learned to become organized by working with a professional organizer for a few months. Once I got the hang of what she was doing, I was able to implement it on my own. If you don't want to work with a professional, ask one of your friends who is particularly organized to come over and show you how they do it. There are also a lot of resources online, especially on YouTube, which can give you great ideas and tips on how to get started.

The basics of organization are that everything has a spot and you don't put stuff away, you put stuff where it goes. A lot of "spots" for things need to be labeled or carved out (like using a bin with different compartments to place different types of items). Once you get into it, I promise that organizing becomes a simple, even enjoyable process, and that you will never want go back.

- **Give Yourself Space and Silence**

In coping with stressors, both small and large, centering myself, imagining myself connecting with nature, and embracing silence helps ground me. This allows me to formulate a plan as to what direction to move in next. This works really well when I am unsure of what to do in a certain situation.

Grounding and giving yourself space and silence is underrated in today's busy world, and is an important factor on the list of ingredients that make up the recipe for success. Something about silence gives your mind the ability to recharge while simultaneously letting your best self (your north star) guide you. It is a technique I employ regularly with both small and large decisions.

- **Be Grateful for Help, Then Pay it Forward**

Success is never gained alone. You might start out alone (most of us do). But eventually, you will need to collaborate with others (whether in your professional or personal life). This means relying on your "team." Success is ultimately a team sport. Every single person who gives you a recommendation, career advice, support, and mentorship, is a critical piece to your success puzzle.

There are two important points I want to mention here. The first is to always show genuine gratitude to those that have helped you along the way. Never forget anyone who has helped you learn or who has helped shape you. It doesn't matter if they're your third-grade teacher, your first boss, or your ex—go back to thank the people who have made you who you are today. The second point is to pay that help forward.

Try and take opportunities to mentor and teach those who are blossoming and growing. The relationship between mentor and mentee is one of the most sacred relationships there is; cherish it, and pass it on to the next generation if you are lucky enough to experience that bond. I am sure you are all familiar with the famous quote, "With great power comes great responsibility." I like to say, "With great mentorship, comes great responsibility to pay it forward."

I hope these tips help you feel healthier and stronger and take you closer to the goal of living life on your terms, every day.

CONCLUSION

To summarize, we have reviewed how to remove barriers and obstacles that had been preventing you from obtaining your dream vision and becoming the ideal version of yourself, then we worked to create your ideal life by defining the ideal you and creating a foundation for a life built on your unique values. The remaining chapters consisted of practical tools and strategies, which are meant to help you quickly and effectively drive your vision forward, making it a genuine reality.

My sincere hope for you in reading this book is that you realize your worth and your power so that you can fully exercise your unique talents and skills in this world, making it a better place (we need it). I hope that I can help ignite the spark inside you just enough to start a real fire and encourage you to make some small changes which lead to big changes, bringing you to your ideal life.

If I had to sum up this book in one message, it's this: you are more powerful than you can even imagine, and it is time to start expressing that power to its fullest extent. Let's go!

AFTERWORD

Sometimes I read a book, become super motivated, and then, a month or so later, I forget about the book (and my newfound motivation). The energy of new ideas and positive changes slowly fade into the ether.

I've been there and that's why I am not leaving you here. I will be providing you with continuing inspiration and resources on my website, social media and through my newsletters. I encourage you to follow me, and check in with me as a way to keep yourself accountable and motivated. If you need my help, or if you have any questions about this program, you can contact me. I love hearing from my readers, and I find that I always seem to have so much in common with those who pick up my book.

If you want to reach out to me, you can email me directly at jen@drjendunphy.com or message me on social media—@drjendunphy. For more content, come visit my website www.drjendunphy.com where you can sign-up for my FREE newsletter, and where you can find studies, blogs, health tools, and more. You can also share your successes, tips, and stories with me.

Don't forget to download the workbook that accompanies this book, so you can have a place to keep all of your answers to the exercises in this book. You can download it at www.drjendunphy.com/books.

If you enjoyed this book, please consider taking a moment to leave an honest review on Amazon.com. It will help people like you find this book and ignite their fire. Thank you.

Made in the USA
Las Vegas, NV
25 August 2024

94398804R00085